Instructor's Manual for

The Informed Argument
Sixth Edition

BY ROBERT P. YAGELSKI AND ROBERT K. MILLER

Prepared by
AMY J. CROUSE-POWERS

THOMSON
TM
WADSWORTH

United States • Australia • Canada • Mexico • Singapore • Spain • United Kingdom

THOMSON
WADSWORTH

The Informed Argument, Sixth Edition, Instructor's Manual
Amy Crouse-Powers

Publisher:	*Michael Rosenberg*
Acquisitions Editor:	*Dickson Musslewhite*
Development Editor:	*Michelle Phifer*
Sr. Production Editor:	*Sally Cogliano*
Director of Marketing:	*Lisa Kimball*
Senior Print Buyer:	*Mary Beth Hennebury*
Compositor/Designer:	*Roberta Landi*
Cover Designer:	*Linda Beaupre*
Printer:	*Webcom*
Cover Image:	*© 2003 Getty Images*

Printed in Canada.
1 2 3 4 5 6   06 05 04 03

For more information contact Wadsworth, 25 Thomson Place, Boston, MA 02210 USA, or you can visit our Internet site at http://www.wadsworth.com

For permission to use material from this text or product contact us:

Tel	1-800-730-2214
Fax	1-800-730-2215
Web	www.thomsonrights.com

ISBN: 0-1550-6984-5

TABLE OF CONTENTS

Preface: Teaching with *The Informed Argument,* Sixth Edition

The Informed Argument, Sixth Edition, provides learning opportunities for a range of learner needs. This book can be used as a reader for a freshman-level to intermediate-level composition course as well as for a critical reading class. The activities in this manual are designed with the needs of first- to second-year college students in mind. To help you plan the logistics of your course, this manual includes the following:

- **points to note**–highlights of each chapter for your quick reference

- **graphic representations** of key points from the text to help provide alternative explanations for more spatial learners

- suggested **class activities** for groups and individuals

- three **sample syllabi.**

INNOVATIVE PEDAGOGICAL FEATURES

The preface to *The Informed Argument* includes a detailed description of the new features of the revised edition. The significant revisions in design and content were made to aid instructors in designing an enjoyable and stimulating course to help students activate the reading and thinking strategies that underlie writing arguments. The innovative design features of the textbook stress the necessity of activating prior knowledge and making connections to related ideas in one's reading. The ready availability of related information in the *Gloss, Context, Sidebar,* and *Complication* boxes aids students in reading carefully and critically.

A Web site to supplement this text is provided. On the Web site for this text (available via http://www.english.wadsworth.com/yagelski/) you will find

- a sample of the supplementary readings that appear in the reader (This section is provided for those who choose to use just the brief edition of the text, but an additional feature is that the works in this section are hyperlinked to other sources of information.)

- a page of annotated external links to Web sites that will provide students a starting point for their own research into current topics

- four case books that provide alternate groupings for readings included in the text along with additional readings that expand the dialectic and provide alternate writing assignments

Teacher to Teacher

My teaching career has been focused on teaching writing, research, and reading to first- and second-year undergraduates at state and community colleges. I bring that perspective to the writing of this manual. I have included a number of asides I call "Teacher to Teacher" in which I share my experiences and my observations about the thinking of first- and second-year students. I offer these ideas only from my experience; they may not be generalizable to the situation in which you work.

Activity

The activity boxes interspersed throughout this manual present ideas that focus on specific rhetorical issues. These are offered as general ideas to adapt to your needs. Mostly, they are activities that have worked well in my own classroom. Usually, I use these activities to draw students' attention to ideas I feel must be emphasized. I find that the time classroom activities require allows students to mull over ideas and apply them in more than one way; classroom activities provide different frames of reference for ideas and typically improve students' comprehension. Activities take time, but the time is typically well spent.

Many of the activities included suggest the use of small groups. Group work is not always easy to manage, which sometimes leads college instructors to avoid it altogether in favor of lectures or whole class discussions. Before you dismiss the use of group work summarily, however, consider that well-managed group work allows all the students in your class the invaluable opportunity to voice their understandings, make corrections for misinterpretation of ideas, learn from their peers, and spend time on task. Conversely, large group discussions only allow one person to speak at a time. And large group discussions are most appropriate for more verbal learners, a category into which the majority of the population does not fall. If you have given up on group work because it hasn't worked for you in the past, perhaps you might take this opportunity to give it one more try.

SOME SUGGESTIONS FOR GROUP ACTIVITIES:

1. Require that the groups produce a specified product. For example, rather than telling groups to "discuss _____," ask them to "make a list of characteristics of _____." You could also prepare discussion questions, have all groups prepare answers to them, and have each group share their answer to one question.

2. Provide specific, written instructions either on a handout, chalkboard, or overhead.

3. Provide carefully defined roles for the members of the group. The more often students work in groups, the more comfortable they become with taking on assigned roles. Some typical roles are

   a. **recorder**—keeps notes for the group

   b. **task master**—is responsible for keeping all members working and on task; also helps ensure that all members are contributing equally

c. **reader**—reads directions and question aloud; this person may also be the **reporter** when the group returns to the larger class group.

4. Give time limits for the work. The group activities described throughout this manual can take a portion of a class period, an entire period, or can extend for longer periods. Let students know how long they have to complete a task. Quite often, giving a relatively short amount of time motivates students to get down to business. Use your judgment.

5. Consider carefully how you will count work produced by groups. Is it for a class participation grade? Will the product be graded for accuracy? Is it possible for students who don't contribute to benefit from the work of others? Tying student grades to the performance of others can present problems. Stories abound about good students who get stuck doing the work of four other classmates because not doing it would harm their own grades. Despite the systems many teachers use that require students to offer feedback on their group's input to the project, students sometimes feel uncomfortable criticizing their peers and still end up short. Consider ways to use group work that make it valuable for students but that don't tie one student's grade to that of another.

Amy Crouse-Powers
State University of New York College at Oneonta

COURSE DESIGN AND SYLLABI

Teacher to Teacher

It has been my experience that freshmen are unaware of the importance of their course syllabi. Walking into a classroom on the first day of the semester, I often see the litter basket filled with syllabi from the class using the room the hour before. If you have freshmen in your class, it is worth your time during the first week to talk to them about the idea of *the syllabus as a contract between teacher and student*. To encourage their overall college success, I emphasize that all their syllabi are important, not just the one for my course.

Setting up a syllabus in a useful format will encourage your students to use it. I usually put an organizer in it for them to record the grades they receive throughout the semester.

Because I find that going over the syllabus in detail is imperative, I don't usually do this on the first day of the semester; I have a number of students added to my class during the first week, and I want to be sure I share this information with as many of my students as I can. I hand out the syllabus on day one and tell them that their homework is to read it. When I go over the syllabus on the second day of class, I ask them to take it out and go through it in detail. Here are some tips:

- Suggest that they take a few notes *on the syllabus* as you go over it.
- Consider telling your students about your *reasons* for such things as your attendance and late work policy.
- Also, let them what assignments you will or not be flexible with.
- Let them know whether they are responsible for the due dates as they are printed or if you are giving *approximate* dates. Each instructor handles this differently.

THINKING ABOUT COURSE DESIGN

Before you begin to put together your class syllabus, take extra time to review closely your institution's purpose and goals for the course. Many departments have a list of general course objectives to provide you with a clear understanding of what is expected of you, and referring to the objectives should eliminate the chance of duplicating course work your students may have had already or will have in the future. If there is no such document outlining the course goals for you, consult the course description in the catalogue or ask a veteran colleague.

When designing your course work assignments, keep in mind that the best way to teach writing and rhetoric is by reinforcing that *writing is a set of interrelated processes.* (See *Instructor's Manual* Chapter 5 for a discussion of writing processes.) For assignments to result in unified, coherent, developed, and technically correct pieces of writing, students must be encouraged to attend to *how* they achieve these qualities. The metacognitive processes a writer goes through, such as asking oneself "What stories can I tell to help show what I mean here?" must be emphasized if not exaggerated for novice writers.

It is of key importance to create a set of clearly defined goals for each writing assignment. I try to think carefully about my assumptions about what students know and don't know before they come to my class. If I am teaching a first-semester freshman-level course, my assumption is that students' range of abilities in writing is wide. So I begin with the very basics: central idea and unified paragraphs. The first time my students write a paper, depending on the course, those two elements may be all I comment on. As we move on throughout the semester and I address more elements of good writing, I hold them accountable for integrating these more advanced skills into their writing. However, because I use portfolios, I have my students go back and revise their first papers to address the more advanced skills they master, such as transitions, introductions, and conclusions, throughout the course.

The content of any piece of writing is ultimately the most important aspect. However, some students misunderstand and assume that grammar is all the teacher is looking for. Every composition instructor has a story of a student who could write a grammatically perfect paper that literally said nothing. Writing and argumentation are more than just using correct grammar, spelling, and punctuation. Students who have been criticized frequently because of errors often become frustrated and unable to write in depth. By focusing on the process rather than the product, you help students express their thoughts with less anxiety. Some ways of helping students understand writing processes include encouraging revision and assigning small group work and collaboration to support the writing of papers.

One way of reinforcing the idea that good writing comes from using the necessary processes is designing the course so that students must create a final portfolio. Portfolios allow students to write and revise, and they also allow the instructor a window into the students' thinking and writing processes. My composition classes use portfolios, but the caveat I offer is to realize that the portfolio approach necessitates that students turn in several papers together to represent their best work. That can represent an inordinate amount of work on your part unless you have a plan for evaluating that work. Portfolios work for me because (a) I have students turn work in repeatedly throughout the semester, so the work in the portfolio is not new to me; (b) I have them turn in all their prior drafts with the current one, so I can see the students' thinking unfolding; and (c) I conference with students. Portfolio assessment simply does not work for some instructors, and that's fine. Fostering the student's understanding and use of the processes required to write well can be done in myriad ways; being conscious and explicit about how you encourage the development of those processes is imperative.

I am providing three syllabi to help you get an idea of how a course might be set up using *The Informed Argument.* The first syllabus is designed for use with the brief edition during a 15-week course. The second is designed for use with the full edition during a 15-week semester. The third is designed for use with the full edition during a 10-week quarter. I have left the readings blank because the themes you and your students are interested in can be introduced in whatever way you want. Readings are easily mixed and matched. If you use one of these syllabi, realize that it may include too much work. It is easier, however, to delete material than to add later. What is presented here is intended to give you ideas for linking concepts and skills through a series of assignments.

Generally, the format and structure of the book can guide your course if it is taken in sequence. For instance, you could develop a 15-week syllabus that provides 1 week for the introduction, 1 week for the section on purposes, 1 week on strategies, 1 week on contexts, 1 week on media, 1 week on constructing, and 9 weeks during which you explore issues from the readings.

Unlike former editions of this text, the reader for this edition presents fairly complex issues throughout and emphasizes the importance of considering the larger context. The arrangement does *not* specifically reflect a progression from simple to complex arguments, so when choosing which issues to assign, you might consider asking students what they are interested in exploring.

SAMPLE SYLLABI

Sample Syllabus #1–15 Weeks for Use with the CONCISE Edition

This syllabus uses readings that are provided on the companion Web site for the text and leaves room for readings from other sources to be integrated into the course. Many small group projects are integrated here both for emphasizing the rhetoric and for encouraging attention to the writing processes.

	In class	Homework students complete before next class period.
Week 1	**Wednesday** • Briefly introduce course. • Hand out syllabus. • Introduce freewriting topic: *What is argument and persuasion? What does it take to be persuaded to change your mind about something?* • Discuss students' freewriting; on the chalkboard, make a list of the assumptions they bring to the discussion. (This could be done in small groups and combined with an ice-breaking activity.) **Friday** • Go over syllabus in detail. • Preview text. • Brainstorm in small groups: What are the purposes of argument in our world?	Read syllabus and bring any questions about it with you to the next class. Read pages 2–5, "An Introduction to Argument." Begin searching for examples of argument. You will need to bring an "argument artifact" by next Wednesday. *(See Chapter 1 in Instructor's Manual for details of this activity.)* Read Chapter 1: The Purposes of Argument. *(Continued on page xii)*

	In class	Homework students complete before next class period.
Week 2	**Monday** • Go over Chapter 1. • Hold class discussion on sidebar "Are Arguments Adversarial?" page 5. **Wednesday** • Have students present and discuss Argument Artifacts on the purposes for the arguments. **Friday** • Finish up "Argument Artifacts." • If you have time, you may want to have a class discussion on one of the issues raised in Chapter 1. (*See Chapter 1 in the* Instructor's Manual *for discussion topic ideas.*)	Read Chapter 2: Strategies for Argument.
Week 3	**Monday** • Go over Chapter 2. • Use "Evaluating Claims and Warrants" activity from Chapter 2. **Wednesday** • Take about 15 minutes to be sure students generally comprehended Hornberger's and Camarota's essays. • Small group activity: Have students evaluate and compare the claims and warrants present in these essays on immigration. Have them share their findings. **Friday** • Have students return to small groups and compare and compile answers to questions on readings. • Go over assignment for essay #1. • Write an argument about immigration in the U.S. • Prewriting on immigration: *What are your reasons for and against immigration?*	Read from Web site: Chapter 11 "Who Gets to Be an American?" Introduction to cluster, Reading #1 Jacob G. Hornberger "Keep the Borders Open," and Reading #2 Steven Camarota "Too Many: Looking Today's Immigration in the Face." Answer questions on Hornberger's and Camarota's essays. Read Chapter 5: Constructing Arguments. Continue prewriting and return to class Monday with list of reasons.

	In class	Homework students complete before next class period.
Week 4	**Monday** • Individual activity: Have students organize ideas from the prewriting considering carefully why they would choose the strategies to employ. *Consider creating visual maps.* • Small group: Have students share organizational plans with the group and discuss how they will proceed. **Wednesday** • Activity: Imagining Your Audience from Chapter 3 in *Instructor's Manual.* • Have students examine drafts with partners, considering the audience's needs. **Friday** • Discuss Chapter 4. • Provide class time for questions on preparation of assignment #1 or peer response.	Draft your argument. Read Chapter 3: The Contexts of Argument. Read Chapter 4: The Media for Argument. Prepare assignment #1 to be turned in.
Week 5	**Monday** • **Assignment #1** due. • Choose an activity from *Instructor's Manual* Chapter 4. **Wednesday** • Discuss "What does it mean to be a good American citizen?" articles. **Friday** • Go over your expectations for assignment #2 on American citizenship. • Introduce prewriting activity for assignment #2.	Read "What does it mean to be a good American Citizen?" cluster on Web site, which includes articles by Russell Baker and Wilfred McClay. Answer questions. Organize and draft assignment #2.
Week 6	**Monday** • Use peer response on assignment #2. **Wednesday** • Assign Chapter 4 Activity: Political Cartoons. **Friday** • **Assignment #2** due. • Hold small or large group discussion using Korten reading questions from Web site.	Read from Web site Korten's "Economies of Meaning" (Chapter 12, Cluster 1). Read from Chapter 12, Cluster 2: Frazier "All Consuming Patriotism," and Deacon "The Joys of Excess." Answer questions. *(Continued on page xiv)*

(Continued on page xiv)

	In class	Homework students complete before next class period.
Week 7	**Monday** • Discuss Frazier's and Deacon's articles. • Go over expectations for assignment #3. • Have class write arguments in which they negotiate differences between those who are concerned about stimulating the economy and those who are concerned with consumer excess. • Prewriting for assignment #3. **Wednesday** • Discuss word choice. (*See* Instructor's Manual *Chapter 5.*) • Use small group work with prewriting and premises. Have students consider word choices appropriate for the audience they intend to reach with this argument. **Friday** • Peer response on assignment #3.	Continue prewriting as needed and come to class with a statement of the main premise to use for this argument. Draft your argument.
Week 8	**Monday** • Take trip to library to learn how the campus catalog system operates. **Wednesday** • Introduce Activity: Evaluating Internet Resources. (*See* Instructor's Manual *Chapter 6.*) **Friday** • **Assignment #3** due. • Discuss reading actively and critically. • Brainstorm for reading techniques with class.	Read Chapter 6: Doing Research. On Web site read introduction to Cluster 3: "How Should Workers be Treated?" and Hightower's "Going Down the Road."
Week 9	**Monday** • Activity: Annotating for research. Annotate "Going down the road" in small groups. • Write 5-minute reflection on the process of annotating: *Was this a method you have used before? How could this method of annotating be of help to you? What did you like or not like about this technique?* **Wednesday** • Activity: Writing Summarizing Effectively Chapter 6 in *Instructor's Manual* (with the article[s] you supply to be summarized). **Friday** • In small groups, have students review the annotations and summaries.. • Have class turn in work at end of class.	On Web site, read "Just Another Hollow Day" by Richards. Annotate and summarize it.

	In class	Homework students complete before next class period.
Week 10	**Monday** • Go over expectations for assignment #4. (This paper topic is chosen by the student and supported with research.) • Large group activity: Generate topics through brainstorming. **Wednesday** • Arrange research in computer lab or library. • Have students turn in statement topic for approval. **Friday** • Lesson: Citing your sources.	Narrow your topic. Read Chapter 7: Documenting Your Sources.
Week 11	**Monday** • Hold writing conferences. **Wednesday** • Hold writing conferences. **Friday** • Hold writing conferences.	Create a plan for assignment #4, draft and revise it.
Week 12	**Monday** • **Assignment #4 due.** • Begin Assignment #5: Class op-ed newsletter or Web site. • Survey the campus or community newspaper for issues of concern. If you or your students have access to an Internet connection, consider expanding this to include issues of national or global concern. • Find several issues, and as a class, briefly discuss the premises underlying the arguments that are made. *Consider whom the issues affect. Consider the purposes for the arguments and how you see yourself participating in the dialectic on the issue.* **Wednesday** • Create a list of topics students would like to consider for inclusion in a class Web site or printed op-ed newsletter. • Vote on issues to be included in class project.	Think about some issues of local concern that you want to generate an argument on. *(Week 12 continued on page xvi)*

	In class	Homework students complete before next class period.
	Friday • Review Chapter 6 section "Conducting Interviews and Surveys." In a large class group, create a survey that will help students generate data to include their projects. • Consider creating the survey so that it can be separated for tallying by small groups.	
Week 13	**Monday** • Administer survey during class time. You might have students go to the student union, cafeteria, etc., to distribute the survey. **Wednesday** • THANKSGIVING BREAK **Friday** • THANKSGIVING BREAK	
Week 14	**Monday** • Activity: Have small groups of students compile data. Have each group tally one section or page of responses (depending on the design of the survey). • Have groups report to the class. **Wednesday** • Discuss data collected and what conclusions could be drawn from it. • Assign prewriting. **Friday** • Allow peer response and revision.	Draft your argument.
Week 15	**Monday** • Proofread in small groups. • **Assignment #5 due.** **Wednesday** • Have class present and share op-ed newsletter. **Friday** • Reflect on students' perception of argumentation and persuasion: *What does it take to persuade you?*	

Assignment #1	10 points	_____
Assignment #2	15 points	_____
Assignment #3	20 points	_____
Assignment #4	25 points	_____
Assignment #5	15 points	_____
Participation in peer response	10 points	_____
Writing conference (preparation and attendance)	5 points	_____
	100 points	_____

Sample Syllabus #2—15 Weeks for Use with the FULL Edition

This syllabus integrates more reading assignments, and the grading scheme requires that students turn in written answers to chapter discussion questions. Other than the prewriting, most of the actual writing would be done outside of class, but for each assignment, there is a writing workshop, in which to emphasize a rhetorical strategy, for peer response or for guided revision.

The reading schedule has been included, but the choices for the readings have been left blank. The reader contains 72 pieces that could be combined in any number of ways. This syllabus calls for students to read between two and four pieces per week, which may be more or less than they can handle. You will have to be the judge of that.

	In class	Homework students complete before next class period.
Week 1	**Wednesday** • Briefly introduce course. • Hand out syllabus. • Freewrite topic: *What is argument and persuasion? What does it take to be persuaded to change your mind about something?* • Discuss freewriting. On the chalk board, make a list of the assumptions students bring to the discussion. This could be done in small groups and combined with an ice-breaking activity. **Friday** • Go over syllabus in detail. • Preview text. • Brainstorm in small groups: *What are the purposes of argument in our world?*	Read syllabus and bring any questions about it with you to the next class. Read pages 2–5, "An Introduction to Argument." Read Chapter 1: The Purposes of Argument. *(Continued on page xviii)*

	In class	Homework students complete before next class period.
Week 2	**Monday** • Go over Chapter 1. • Hold class discussion on sidebar on page 5, "Are Arguments Adversarial?" **Wednesday** • Discuss reading actively and critically. • Go over Chapter 2. • Use "Evaluating Claims and Warrants" Activity from Chapter 2 of *Instructor's Manual*. **Friday** • Work in small groups to answer discussion questions. • Return to large group to report answers.	Read Chapter 2: Strategies for Argument. Read Chapter XX Cluster X Introduction and Readings X and X. Read Chapter XX Cluster X Introduction and Readings X and X.
Week 3	**Monday** • Class will work in small groups to answer discussion questions. • Have them return to large group to report answers. **Wednesday** • Go over assignment for essay #1. • Assign prewriting. **Friday** • Discuss planning and revising. • Spend time during class talking about ways of assessing logic, relevance, and sufficiency of details. Have students work in pairs to revise content. • Collect ROUGH DRAFTS to be returned on Monday.	Read Chapter 5: Constructing Arguments. Organize and draft paper.
Week 4	**Monday** • Organize writing workshop for assignment #1. **Wednesday** • **Assignment #1** due. • Activity: "Imagining Your Audience" from Chapter 3 in *Instructor's Manual*. **Friday** • Go over Chapter 3.	Read Chapter 3: The Contexts of Argument. Read Chapter X Cluster X Reading X. Answer questions.
Week 5	**Monday** • Discuss readings, focusing on contexts. • Go over assignment for essay #2. • Assign prewriting.	Read Chapter 4: Media for Arguments. Organize and draft assignment #2.

	In class	Homework students complete before next class period.
	Wednesday • Discuss Chapter 4. • Chapter 4 Activity: Political Cartoons. **Friday** * Begin writing workshop for assignment #2.	Read Chapter X Cluster X Readings X and X. Answer questions.
Week 6	**Monday** • **Assignment #2 due.** • Discuss readings. **Wednesday** • Take trip to library to learn how campus catalog system operates. **Friday** • Use information literacy activity from Chapter 6 in *Instructor's Manual*.	Read Chapter 6: Doing Research. Read Chapter 7: Documenting Your Sources.
Week 7	**Monday** • Go over expectations for Assignment #3. Assign prewriting. **Wednesday** • Discuss readings. **Friday** • Explain lesson: "Citing Sources" and "Avoiding Plagiarism." Begin writing workshop.	Read Chapter X Cluster X Readings X and X. Answer questions. Read Chapter X Cluster X Readings X and X. Answer questions.
Week 8	**Monday** • **Assignment #3 due.** • Discuss readings. **Wednesday** • Discuss readings. **Friday** • Assign activity: "Annotating for Research." Annotate article in small groups. • Write 5-minute reflection on the process of annotating: *Was this a method you have used before? How could this method of annotating help you? What did you like or not like about this technique?*	Read Chapter X Cluster X Readings X and X. Answer questions. Read Chapter X Cluster X Readings X and X. Answer questions.

(Continued on page xx)

	In class	Homework students complete before next class period.
Week 9	**Monday** • Assign activity: "Summarizing Effectively," Chapter 6 in *Instructor's Manual*. Use readings that were assigned for homework for this activity. **Wednesday** • Go over expectations for assignment #4. • Assign prewriting. • Discuss reading. **Friday** • Begin writing workshop.	Read Chapter X Cluster X Readings X and X. Answer questions.
Week 10	**Monday** • **Assignment #4 due.** • Go over expectations for Assignment #5. • Assign prewriting. **Wednesday** • Discuss reading. **Friday** • Assign writing workshop.	Read Chapter X Cluster X Readings X and X. Answer questions. Read Chapter X Cluster X Readings X and X. Answer questions.
Week 11	**Monday** • **Assignment #5 due.** • Discuss reading. **Wednesday** • Go over expectations for Research Assignment #1. * Discuss how to organize a large research project. • Brainstorm for topics. **Friday** • Take trip to computer lab or library to begin students' researching. • Use supplemental Web site to begin searching.	Write a statement of the topic you intend to cover in your research paper.
Week 12	**Monday** • Return to lab to continue research. • Set up individual conferences during lab time to discuss topics. **Wednesday** • Discuss readings. **Friday** • Initiate writing workshop.	Read Chapter X Cluster X Readings X and X. Answer questions.

	In class	Homework students complete before next class period.
Week 13	**Monday** • **Assignment #6** due. • Write a reflection on the experience of writing the researched argument: *Consider what went well, what problems you encountered, what you will do differently next time.* **Wednesday** • THANKSGIVING BREAK FRIDAY • THANKSGIVING BREAK	Read Chapter X Cluster X Readings X and X. Answer questions.
Week 14	**Monday** • Discuss readings. • Go over expectations for Research Assignment #2. • Brainstorm for topics. **Wednesday** • Take trip to computer lab or library to begin researching. • Use supplemental Web site. **Friday** • Return to lab to continue research. • Hold individual conferences during lab time to discuss topics.	Read Chapter X Cluster X Readings X and X. Answer questions.
Week 15	**Monday** • Discuss readings. **Wednesday** • Hold writing workshop. **Friday** • **Assignment #7** due. • Students reflect on perception of argumentation and persuasion: *What does it take to persuade you?*	

GRADING SCALE

Assignment #1	5 points	_____
Assignment #2	10 points	_____
Assignment #3	10 points	_____
Assignment #4	10 points	_____
Assignment #5	10 points	_____
Assignment #6 (researched)	20 points	_____
Assignment #7 (researched)	20 points	_____
Homework (written answers to discussion questions)	5 points	_____
	100 points	_____

Sample Syllabus #3–10 Weeks for Use with the FULL Edition

This is a pared-down version of the 15-week syllabus. This one incorporates a portfolio approach.

	In class	Homework students complete before next class period.
Week 1	**Monday** • Briefly introduce course. • Hand out syllabus. • Assign freewriting topic: *What is argument and persuasion? What does it take to be persuaded to change your mind about something?*	Read syllabus and bring any questions about it with you to next class.
	Wednesday • Discuss freewriting—on the chalkboard, make a list of assumptions students bring to the discussion. (This could be done in small groups and combined with an ice-breaking activity.) • Go over syllabus in detail. • Preview text.	Read pages 2–5, "An Introduction to Argument."
	Friday • Have students brainstorm in small groups: *What are the purposes of argument in our world?*	Read Chapter 1: The Purposes of Argument.
Week 2	**Monday** • Go over Chapter 1. • Discuss sidebar with class, "Are Arguments Adversarial?"	Read Chapter 2: Strategies for Argument.
	Wednesday • Discuss reading actively and critically. • Go over Chapter 2. • Use "Evaluating Claims and Warrants" activity from Chapter 2.	Read Chapter 6: Doing Research. Read Chapter 7: Documenting Your Sources.
	Friday • Take trip to library to learn how campus catalog system operates.	Read Chapter 5: Constructing Arguments.
Week 3	**Monday** • Discuss Chapter 5. • Go over assignment for essay #1, which should include two sources. • Assign prewriting.	

	In class	Homework students complete before next class period.
	Wednesday • Examine citing sources and avoiding plagiarism. • Discuss planning and revising. **Friday** • Teach peer response technique. • Spend time during class talking about ways of assessing logic, relevance, and sufficiency of details. Have students work in peer response pairs to revise content.	Organize and draft paper.
Week 4	**Monday** • **Assignment #1 due.** • Assign activity "Imagining Your Audience" from Chapter 3 in *Instructor's Manual.* **Wednesday** • Go over Chapter 3. • Go over assignment for essay #2. • Assign prewriting.	Read Chapter 3: The Contexts of Argument. Read Chapter X Cluster X Reading X. Answer questions.
Week 5	**Monday** • Use "Reading Actively and Critically." **Wednesday** • Assign writing summaries. **Friday** • Establish writing workshop.	Read Chapter X Cluster X Readings X and X.
Week 6	**Monday** • **Assignment #2 due.** • Use "Annotating for Research." *(See Chapter 6.)* **Wednesday** • Discuss Chapter 4. • Assign chapter 4 Activity: Political Cartoons. **Friday** • Discuss readings.	Read Chapter 4: The Media for Argument. Read Chapter X Cluster X Readings X and X. Answer questions.
Week 7	**Monday** • Go over expectations for Assignment #3. • Assign prewriting.	Read Chapter X Cluster X Readings X and X. Answer questions. *(Week 7 continued on page xxiv)*

	In class	Homework students complete before next class period.
	Wednesday • Discuss readings. **Friday** • Begin writing workshop.	Read Chapter X Cluster X Readings X and X.
Week 8	**Monday** • **Assignment #3** due. • Discuss readings. **Wednesday** • Go over expectations for Assignment #4. • Begin prewriting.	Read Chapter X Cluster X Readings X and X.
Week 9	**Monday** • Set up writing workshop. **Wednesday** • **Assignment #4** due. • Discuss readings **Friday** • Begin writing workshop for portfolios: *Portfolios should include all four essays in revised form and an introductory essay that explains the process you used to achieve the products you have included.*	Read Chapter X Cluster X Readings X and X. Answer questions. Read Chapter X Cluster X Readings X and X. Answer questions.
Week 10	**Monday** • Discuss reading. **Wednesday** • **Portfolios** due. **Friday** • Have class present portfolios.	

GRADING SCALE

Portfolio containing four revised essays and introduction	60 points	_____
Homework	30 points	_____
Presentation	5 points	_____
Participation	5 points	_____
	100 points	_____

Introduction to the Course

PREVIEWING THE TEXT

As an instructor, you choose a text based on the features it offers. Students, however, choose a text because someone has assigned it to them. Share with your students the reasons you made the choice you did so that they understand the purpose behind their reading.

The Informed Argument has been designed to aid students in their reading. The articles are supplemented with information that will allow them to make the schematic connections necessary to aid their comprehension. Use class time to help students preview the structures of the text. If you are using the full edition, point out the differences between the rhetoric portion in the front and the reader in the back. You can also help them examine features such as the introductions, four kinds of supplementary boxes, and questions for discussion in the reader; this activity will likely lead to a discussion on what will be expected of them when they read.

ASSESSING READING LEVEL

Readings in this text vary in length and difficulty. Because the uses for this text are many, the instructor should carefully consider how the readings will match the needs of the students before assigning them. One way to assess the difficulty of any piece is by scanning or typing a few paragraphs of the piece into Microsoft Word and then using the spell check function under the Tools menu to check the readability statistics. This is a box that "pops up" after running spell check if you have chosen that option. The Flesch-Kincaid Grade Level, which is based on word and sentence sophistication, gives an idea of the necessary reading ability a student would need to easily comprehend the writing. A Flesch-Kincaid grade level of 11.6, for example, means that the student would need an 11th-grade sixth-month reading ability to comprehend the writing.

For more information about how to select the readability statistics, check the Help menu on your word processing program.

DEALING WITH DIFFICULT READINGS

As a reading teacher, I never shy away from using sophisticated readings. I steadfastly believe that students need to be exposed to readings that challenge them. The key, however, is that they must be supported in order to read successfully. One way I support their reading of more difficult pieces is by reading aloud to the entire class while they follow along in the text. Learners are often able to process aurally that which they cannot process by reading because spoken inflection aids comprehension.

Other methods of supporting comprehension, such as annotating, summarizing, and paraphrasing, are described in this book.

Part I: Understanding Argument

This short introduction helps students see the rhetorical definition of argument and recognize examples of argument in their daily lives. Specifically, it introduces the focus of the book: argumentation is "engaging with others to address problems" (3).

Beginning the course by having students examine their own understandings of argument is usually a good starting point, and this introductory reading would work well to follow an in-class freewriting that allows them to explore their assumptions about argumentation.

Activity: **Argument on Artifacts**

Revealing how argument shapes our everyday lives is a good way to begin a course that uses *The Informed Argument*, Sixth Edition. The introduction to Part I provides a springboard to help students see how argument works in their own lives. In the first week of the course, assign "An Introduction to Argument," and then have students bring an artifact to class that demonstrates the existence of argument in their own communities. Students can bring in video- or audio-taped segments of arguments from TV or radio or photocopies of letters to the editor. They can share these in small groups or with the whole class and discuss the ways in which argument affects their daily lives.

Activity: **Class Discussion on "Truth"**

Use the sidebar "Are Arguments Adversarial?" on page 5 to generate a discussion on the nature of truth. Have students form small groups and create a list of the requisite qualities for something to be true. Discussing such an abstraction may not be easy for some students, so this activity will likely require that you circulate among the students as they work. After they've generated their lists, have the groups compare their ideas with the whole class to find the commonalities between their responses. (One possibly easy way of having groups share their lists is by having them write the lists on overhead transparencies.)

Part I: An Introduction to Argument

1 The Purposes of Argument

This short chapter provides students with the necessary background to understand how arguments prove useful in our society. The broad purposes for argument are introduced with brief examples:

- to inquire
- to assert
- to dominate
- to negotiate differences

Activity: **Class Discussion on "Truth"**

After assigning this chapter, have students re-examine the "argument artifacts" they brought to class to determine possible purposes the authors had in mind when offering their arguments.

POINTS TO NOTE

Students are often unfamiliar with the idea of argumentation as anything other than simple disagreement. Outlined here are the most important points from Chapter 1. Highlighting these for the students will help them decode the text and reinforce the purpose of the chapter.

This chapter expands the idea of the uses for argument: argumentation is for solving problems, not just for getting one's own way.

ARGUMENTS TO ASSERT (PAGE 11)

- "Traditionally, argument has been understood as a formal attempt to state a position on an issue (your thesis), offer acceptable reasons for that position, provide evidence in support of those reasons, and anticipate objections. Indeed, to write an effective argument of any kind requires you to make a clear assertion and support it adequately" (12).

ARGUMENTS TO INQUIRE (PAGE 13)

An important idea here is that inquiry is the nature of almost all academic writing. Drawing attention to this point may help emphasize the larger applicability of this course.

- Inquiry is "arguing to learn and understand" (13).

- "These arguments, then, are exploratory in two ways: (a) they encourage the writer to explore a topic in order to arrive at a reasonable position; and (b) they invite writers to engage in exploring that topic as well" (16).

Activity: **Examining Bolter Excerpt**

Discuss the excerpt from Jay David Bolter's *Writing Space* that appears on pages 14–15. How can you tell that this is an argument to inquire? What is the difference between this writing and writing that is intended to simply assert a point? Pay careful attention to the choices of words the author has made.

ARGUMENTS TO DOMINATE (PAGE 16)

Arguments that dominate are used in "win-lose" situations and are particularly applicable in situations involving the law.

- "Being able to recognize the complexity of . . . situations will help you identify arguments to dominate so that you can make informed decisions about them" (17–18).

Examples provided in the text note that sometimes truth is not what is emphasized as much as what is morally or ethically relevant.

ARGUMENTS TO NEGOTIATE AND RECONCILE (PAGE 18)

Arguments that negotiate differences lead to compromise.

- Writers practicing **Rogerian argument** negotiate differences by "restat[ing] what others have said before offering their own views" (19). This style of argumentation "rests on the assumption that language can be completely neutral—an idea that has been seriously questioned by modern linguists and philosophers" (19).

Activity: **Discussion on Neutrality of Language**

On page 19, the point is raised that "Rogers envisioned situations in which individuals are engaged in dialogue, and his commitment to the importance of restating others' ideas (without evaluating them) rests on the assumption that language can be completely neutral." This point is worth considering with your students. Ask your students to consider the role of language in our society. Is language ever neutral? Is listening to the other side of an issue always effective? These broad questions can help you lead students to see the role of argument in shaping what we do and what we believe as a society.

In small groups, have students make up some scenarios for how the Rogerian model of communication could come into play in their world. You might spur their thinking with some issues of local concern, such as a dispute on your campus on how to use student association funds or whether tuition should be raised. Discuss the merits and detriments of the Rogerian model of communication in the realm of argument. Spending time considering practical applications of this method will likely help students choose to use this method appropriately when it is needed in their writing.

2 Strategies for Argument

Having students begin to discuss reading argument at this point could work well. Pairing readings that demonstrate the language uses described in this chapter with activities specifically focused on those nuances will aid students in comprehending the rhetorical ideas.

Help students understand the purpose for reading this chapter by pointing out that these strategies are about the choices writers make, usually *prior to* drafting their arguments. These strategies are usually activated after the initial prewriting and through the drafting and revising stages of writing. Also, draw students' attention to the idea that the purpose for their argument—either to dominate, to inquire, to assert, or to negotiate differences—will probably help drive their choices of strategy.

POINTS TO NOTE

ARISTOTLE

Realize that most freshmen haven't taken an introductory philosophy class, so you might want to provide some background on who Aristotle was and why we still refer to him. One good source of information is the *Internet Encyclopedia of Philosophy* located at http://www.utm.edu/research/iep/a/aristotl.htm.

LOGICAL ARGUMENTS (PAGE 24)

The extent to which you teach logic is your own choice. For many, however, teaching logic is of secondary importance to teaching the basic principles of writing: supporting a clearly defined thesis, anticipating opposition, making concessions, treating opponents with respect, and using sources responsibly. With this in mind, you may best teach logic by examining specific readings during your class discussions. Consider carefully the choices writers have made when crafting their arguments during these discussions. Further, requiring students to write an inductive or deductive piece isn't recommended. It is better to emphasize that different kinds of reasoning provide choices that writers can make for themselves—and that these choices can be combined.

The model of logic employed by classical rhetoricians is ancient. This section cites the three classical elements of argumentation: *ethos, pathos,* and *logos.* Focusing on these elements with students can help them see that an argument does not depend on logic alone—and that argument can fail to achieve its purpose if, for example, a writer appears arrogant or belligerent.

Some students find it easier to make appeals to emotion than to make appeals to reason. So, while recognizing that pathos can play an important role in argument, you may want to caution students not to rely too heavily on it, as heavily emotional arguments are more easily refuted. When discussing ethos, you might look ahead to the material on evaluating sources. You might also ask students to consider whether ethos can be artificially achieved through skill with words (as Aristotle believed) or whether credibility cannot be faked (as Quintilian believed). Finally, a discussion of ethos can be used to remind students that you should always be careful to treat both your audience and your opponents with respect. Few people are likely to be converted to your view if you treat them as if they are fools and dismiss their beliefs with contempt.

■ Logos (lŏg′ŏs′, lō′gōs′) *n.* (definition from Dictionary.com) as defined in the field of "*Philosophy*. a. In pre-Socratic philosophy, the principle governing the cosmos, the source of this principle, or human reasoning about the cosmos. b. Among the Sophists, the topics of rational argument or the arguments themselves. c. In Stoicism, the active, material, rational principle of the cosmos. Identified with God, it is the source of all activity and generation and is the power of reason residing in the human soul."

■ "Logical argument . . . is made objectively on the basis of facts or reason rather than emotion" (24).

■ "The effectiveness of a logical argument depends in large part on whether or not the main assumption—usually called the *main premise* in formal logic—is valid or acceptable" (25).

■ "Arguments rarely rely on logic alone, but we tend to think of reason as being superior to emotion when it comes to argumentation" (25).

REASONING INDUCTIVELY

Inductive: "Drawing conclusions based on specific evidence" (25)

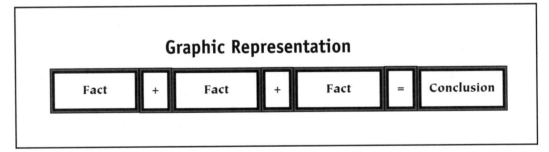

REASONING DEDUCTIVELY

Deductive: "When an argument rests on a fundamental truth, right, or value, rather than on available evidence" (26).

■ **Premise**—"the truth, right, or belief from which a writer deduces an argument."

1. It should be general enough that an audience is likely to accept it, thus establishing a common ground between writer and audience.

2. It should be specific enough to prepare the way for the argument that will follow" (28).

- "What makes formulating a good premise difficult is that a premise usually refers to or invokes fundamental values or beliefs that we don't often examine consciously" (28).

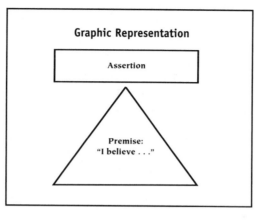

- **Syllogism**—"a three-part argument in which the conclusion rests on two premises, the first of which is the ***major premise*** because it is the main assumption on which the argument rests" (28).

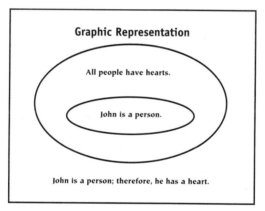

- **The Enthymeme** (ĕn'thə-mēm')—"informal logic in arguments," is "a syllogism that consists of only two parts" because one is implied (29).

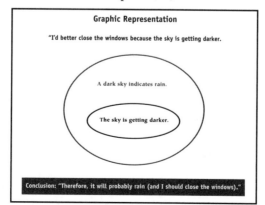

Activity: Becoming Information Literate

News sources often reflect not only a political agenda but also a cultural one. A cultural agenda may be less apparent to those who share in a view of the world sculpted by national cultural norms. Choose a current event from this week's news in the U.S. Using *The Informed Argument*, Sixth Edition's Web site, have students find articles about that event from several of the sites provided under the "General News Sources from the U.S. and Abroad" portion of the site, making sure they choose at least two sources from outside the U.S. Compare the presentation of the information across the sources. Ask students to consider the slant and word choice of the writers. One way of doing this is for students to use a graphic organizer for their thinking, such as the one below:

Unique to Article #1	Similarities	Unique to Article #2

After completing this analysis, reflect on the similarities and differences you found.

See also the activity titled "Examining Cultural Differences" in Part I Chapter 3 of this manual.

THE TOULMIN MODEL OF ARGUMENTATION

- "Toulmin's model includes three main components: the claim, the data or reasons, and the warrant. According to Toulmin, the basis of all arguments is the claim, which is the writer's (or speaker's) statement of belief—the conclusion or point he or she wishes to prove. The *data* or *reasons* are the evidence or information a writer or speaker offers to support that claim. And the *warrant* is a general statement that establishes a trustworthy relationship between the data and the claim; it is a fundamental assumption . . . on which a claim can be made and supported" (31).

UNDERSTANDING CLAIMS AND WARRANTS

Claims and Warrants can both come under dispute because they are complex and depend on a range of variables. Claims can be supported by a variety of data, so the type of support chosen should match the writing situation. Because they are generalizations, warrants will not necessarily provide a solid base upon which undisputed arguments can rest.

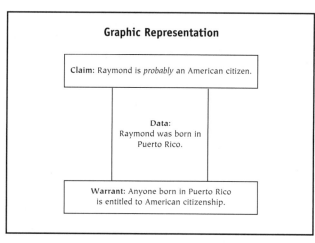

Graphic Representation

Claim: Raymond is *probably* an American citizen.

Data:
Raymond was born in
Puerto Rico.

Warrant: Anyone born in Puerto Rico
is entitled to American citizenship.

Activity: **Evaluating Claims and Warrants**

Use the section with this title that appears on pages 33–35 of the text to complete this activity. In groups of two to four, students can visit an opinion-editorial Web site, such as ones for the *New York Times* (http://www.nytimes.com/pages/opinion/) and *The Wall Street Journal* (http:// www.opinionjournal.com/) and find an argument that uses the Toulmin model of argumentation. Ask them to answer the following:

1. What is the claim that underlies the argument?
2. What is the warrant that underlies the argument?
3. What is the intended audience for this writing?

FALLACIES (PAGE 35)

Dwelling too long on logical fallacies can make students feel that it is impossible to write a logical argument. Therefore, you may want to limit this section's emphasis by referring to it as these fallacies crop up in readings. Or it may be wise to focus on the most frequently found flaws, such as ad hominem arguments, jumping to conclusions, and the slippery slope.

- **Appealing to Pity** (also called "Sob Story"). "You should be skeptical of any appeal to pity that is irrelevant to the conclusion or that seems designed to distract attention from the other factors you should be considering."

- **Appealing to Prejudice.** These arguments are fallacious "when couched in inflammatory language or when offered as a crowd-pleasing device to distract attention from whether the case at hand is reasonable and well-informed."

- **Appealing to Tradition.** This appeal "is fallacious when tradition becomes the only reason for justifying a position."

- **Arguing by Analogy** (also called "False Comparison"). "You must first be sure that the things you are comparing have several characteristics in common and that these similarities are relevant to the conclusion you intend to draw."

- **Attacking the Character of Opponents** (also called "*ad hominem*"). This approach uses "personal attacks on opponents while ignoring what they have to say, or distracting attention from it"

- **Attributing False Causes** (also called "*post hoc*"). This argument assumes "an event is the result of something that merely occurred before it."

- **Attributing Guilt by Association.** "Nothing specific has been argued, but a negative association has been either created or suggested through hints and innuendos."

- **Begging the Question** (also called "circular reasoning"). The "writer begins with a premise that is acceptable only to anyone who will agree with the conclusion that is subsequently reached."

- **Equivocating.** This argument uses "vague or ambiguous language to mislead an audience."

- **Ignoring the Question** (also called "Red Herring"). The speaker or writer talks about something completely off the topic to turn the audience's attention from the matter at hand.

- **Jumping to Conclusions.** "The conclusion in question has not been supported by an adequate amount of evidence."

- **Opposing a Straw Man.** This approach occurs when "arguers . . . pretend that they are responding to the views of their opponents when they are only setting up a type of artificial opposition which they can easily refute."

- **Presenting a False Dilemma.** "A speaker or writer poses a choice between two alternatives while overlooking other possibilities and implying that other possibilities do not exist."

- **Reasoning That Does Not Follow** (also called "*non sequitur*"). "A conclusion does not follow logically from the explanation given for it."

- **Sliding down a Slippery Slope.** An argument asserts that "one step will inevitably lead to an undesirable second step."

Activity: Fallacies

Have students in small groups choose a fallacy and make up an argument that purposely employs that type of fallacious reasoning. Students might create a visual aid, a skit, or a short speech to present their ideas. These can either be serious or funny. Have students present their arguments and have the class explain what's wrong with the arguments. This is an activity that requires the students to become "experts" on one type of fallacy in order to teach it to the class; this experience is likely to make the fallacies more memorable than simply reading about them or locating them in others' arguments.

EMOTIONAL ARGUMENTS (PAGE 41)

Pathos (pā'thŏs', -thôs) n. (1) A quality, as of an experience or a work of art, that arouses feelings of pity, sympathy, tenderness, or sorrow. (2) The feeling, as of sympathy or pity, so aroused. (3) This section presents the idea that emotional arguments are often easily refuted because of the complex nature of human emotion." (Dictionary.com)

Examples in this section point out the use of connotative language that could evoke opposite responses depending upon the audience.

CHARACTER-BASED ARGUMENTS (PAGE 43)

Ethos "(ē'thŏs') n. The disposition, character, or fundamental values peculiar to a specific person, people, culture, or movement." (Dictionary.com)

This section points out the complicated nature of the invocation of the character of either the writer of the argument or that of someone else who has participated in the dialogue on this issue.

3 The Contexts of Argument

"No matter what kind of argument you wish to make, no matter what your purpose, there are at least three main contexts you should consider as you construct an argument:

- the rhetorical situation

- the cultural context

- and the particular moment in which we are arguing, which we can call the historical context" (54)

POINTS TO NOTE

THE RHETORICAL SITUATION (PAGE 54)

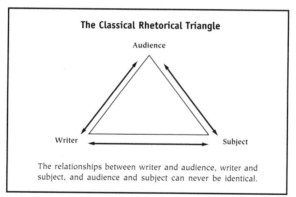

The Classical Rhetorical Triangle

Audience

Writer

Subject

The relationships between writer and audience, writer and subject, and audience and subject can never be identical.

ANALYZING YOUR AUDIENCE

Audience is also addressed in Chapter 5. Refer to Chapter 5 notes in this manual for more on this topic.

1. "Try to determine what you may already know about your intended audience" (55).

    - Sometimes an audience will be very specific and have specialized knowledge of the problem or situation you intend to address.

    - Other times the audience will be far more general, so "you can approach such an audience in a way that is likely to engage a majority of readers" (56).

2. Assume "an intelligent and fair-minded audience" (56).

3. Imagining "a skeptical audience will enable you to anticipate and respond to opposing views or objections to your position, thus building a stronger case" (56).

   • Consider whether your audience is likely to generally agree or disagree with you.

Teacher to Teacher

Having students consider their audience's needs is integral to any writing course because writing that fails to consider its audience is writing that can be neither relevant nor sufficient in its development. Many problems with writing stem from the writer's inability to recognize that what is in his or her head is not accessible to those who read the details chosen for the writing.

Activity: Imagining Your Audience

Give students a topic that is of local concern to them. If you are on a residential campus that has limited parking, for example, the topic might be an argument for a different system to determine who is allowed to park on campus. If you are on a nonresidential campus (and parking is not a sufficient problem to spark students' imaginations), consider using a topic such as the cost of food in the dining halls.

Alone or in groups, have students write a two- to three-sentence-proposal for a solution to this problem. Then, have them answer the following questions about their imagined audience:

1. Where would this argument appear?

2. Given this context, will my audience have general or specific experience to bring to this topic?

3. Is it best to assume that only students will read this argument or that those in power will also read it? In other words, who are **not** your readers?

4. Who would agree with my solution? Who would disagree?

5. Is my solution to this problem fair to everyone? What is a situation that would make my solution unfair (even if it is only for one person)?

6. Why would someone be skeptical about this solution? What can I do to take their misgivings into account?

CULTURAL CONTEXT (PAGE 58)

Culture comprises, among other things, national origin, gender, sexual orientation, and age. These categories intertwine in innumerable ways, so it is incumbent upon the writer to consider at least who one is and to whom he or she is writing. The examples given in this section show the ways in which writers reveal their own lives and how that unveiling may be received by those whose cultures and experiences differ either subtly or dramatically from that of the writer.

One typically successful way of revealing cultural differences to students is to have them examine what makes up their own profiles in the way that Brian Fay does in the excerpt on page 59. (Consider carefully whether this lesson should be undertaken before or after your students have read this excerpt. You might even want to insert the reading between their brainstorming, and the follow-up reflective writing for this activity.) You might begin this lesson by introducing the word *bias* and claiming that it is neither necessarily positive nor negative. Bias is a result of an individual's experiences; it is his or her way of understanding the world. Help students examine their own biases by asking them to answer the following:

1. What is your religion?
2. What is your social class?
3. What is your political affiliation?
4. Where did you grow up?
5. What was an event in your life that makes you look at people differently?
6. What is your position in the family? (How many children are there in your family?)
7. What is your gender?

Many questions can work well here. Each one of these autobiographical facts adds a filter through which a person sees the world. Use students' answers as a jumping-off point for discussing how these experiences add to their way of seeing the world.

Another way to go about this activity is to have students complete the statement "I am . . ." several times. You can even model this before they begin so they get an idea of how to proceed (e.g., I am American. I am a woman.).

FOLLOW-UP: Reflective Writing After discussing these categories, have students read through several letters to the editor from your local newspaper to find one to which they have a particularly strong reaction and discuss how it affects them as readers. Ask what part of their own backgrounds makes them react in the ways they do. This activity could either be done in small groups or as a written homework assignment.

HISTORICAL CONTEXT (PAGE 65)

- **Kairos**—"The ancient Greek rhetoricians used the term *kairos* to describe an opportune moment for making a specific argument or trying to persuade an audience to act in a specific situation" (65).

- "The time in which an argument is made can profoundly affect not only how an audience might react to it but also its very meaning and import" (66). The Declaration of Independence is the example used to illustrate the differences in how it was received at the time it was written and how it is received today. Any political speech would typically fall into this category.

4 The Media for Argument

This chapter focuses on the ways in which media affect the delivery and even the content of argument. Of course, the advent of the Internet and library technologies impacts this discussion in ways we never dreamed just ten years ago. (And remember, many of our students have never known an academic world without these technologies!)

Activity: Close Reading of George Will Excerpt

Attending to students' reading abilities is imperative in this course because the more proficient students are at reading, the clearer their writing will become. For many students, the excerpt on page 69 will be difficult to comprehend, although they are unlikely to let you know that they are experiencing any difficulty. This reading presents an excellent opportunity to demonstrate the metacognitive skills that proficient readers use to decode language.

Before assigning this chapter, make a transparency of the George Will piece and display it for the students. (The text is available in large font at the end of this chapter.) Read the passage aloud to students and lead them in a discussion about how each phrase relates to the others to make meaning. After determining that the students understand how the ideas fit together, lead them to answer the question, "Let's restate this idea in simpler language. What's Will saying here?"

POSSIBLE PARAPHRASE: Will is saying that to ensure their own power, evil political entities in the world dismiss the existence of human nature, which allows these entities to dominate people and reduce them to violence.

These are the best of times for the worst of people. And for **the toxic idea** at the core of all the most *murderous ideologies* of the modern age. That idea is that **human nature** is, if not a fiction, at least so **watery and flimsy** that it poses no serious impediment to evil political entities determined to *treat people* as malleable clay to be molded into creatures at once **submissive and violent**.

ANALYZING ARGUMENTS IN PRINT (PAGE 70)

This section considers the effect of the printed word on argument.

Activity: Printed vs. Spoken Language

Most students will not have considered that print is not a "natural" medium or that it really differs from speech. You might demonstrate this by having them compare written and spoken arguments for the ways in which language is used. Have them consider use of rhetorical pattern, sentence length, syntax, word choice, and complexity of ideas. You could use examples generated by the Argument Artifact activity described in Chapter 1 of this manual or compare a transcript of a speech with a written argument by the same individual.

READING ARGUMENTS CRITICALLY

This section relates the discussion of audience from Chapter 3 to how to read arguments. Be very careful to define the word *critical* with your students and be sure each of them understands that it is not a simple equivalent of "disapprove of."

- "Reading critically means looking carefully at the way a writer tries to address a specific audience for a specific publication; it means being aware of how your own perspective, beliefs, and values might influence your reaction to particular arguments" (73).

EVALUATING *ETHOS*

- "You may not identify with the writer—or with the audience he or she directly addresses— or you may not wish to identify with the writer" (73–74). Argument often provides uncomfortable reading because it can challenge that which we hold dear.

The idea of being a resisting reader is one that might help students see the importance of reading widely in order to be able to most effectively participate in a larger dialogue. Judith Fetterley coined the term *resisting reader* (*The Resisting Reader: A Feminist Approach to American Fiction*, Bloomington 1978) to describe a reader–response approach which calls readers to challenge texts they encounter rather than simply "assenting" to them.

- Ways to analyze and evaluate a writer's ethos (74–75):
  1. Notice with which group the writer identifies—either implicitly or explicitly. How do you react to this?
  2. Notice the tone or "sound" of the voice that comes from the writing. (You might try reading aloud.) How do you react to this?
  3. Notice how the writer uses evidence to support the contention that is made. Does the evidence feel complete to you? Would you feel the same if your own position on the issue was different?

4. Attempt to state the values that underlie the writer's argument. Are these values the same as yours?

APPRAISING EVIDENCE

- "Almost anything can be used as evidence: statistics, opinions, observations, theories, anecdotes . . . Moreover, what counts as appropriate and persuasive evidence always depends upon context" (76).

FACTS AS EVIDENCE

- "What counts as a fact and what is considered ample evidence depend on context and audience" (77).

- "As a reader, you should pay close attention to *how* a writer is using evidence as well as to what evidence is presented" (78).

PERSONAL EXPERIENCE AS EVIDENCE

- "The extent to which readers will find such first-hand evidence compelling will vary" depending on the context and the number of other questions the experience raises in the reader (79).

AUTHORITY AS EVIDENCE

- Note whether the authority's ideas are being quoted in statistical form or in interpreted, theoretical form, as in the example from David Orr on page 79.

- Citing a well-known authority or expert can help the writer capitalize on "an established credibility."

This section provides another opportunity to discuss how knowledge is constructed and disseminated.

VALUES AS EVIDENCE

- "If you invoke a principle or value that your readers may not share, your evidence will not be very persuasive to them and your argument may be weakened. In addition, values and beliefs can be open to interpretation, just like factual evidence or personal experience" (80–81).

Differentiating between values and fact is important.

PRESENTING EVIDENCE IN VISUAL FORM

- A visual representation of data can often convey more information more dramatically than text.

- "Evidence presented visually . . . can be appealing and persuasive, but it should be subject to the same careful scrutiny that you would use to assess any evidence" (82).

You might consider asking students to include a visual element with one of their arguments.

Proficient readers of argument are keen to the ways in which information can be presented in misleading ways. Although graphs and charts can often provide information more efficiently, they can also easily mislead readers. Gather together some examples of recent articles that provide charts or graphs. (*USA Today* always uses charts and graphs.) Choose some that appear to use visual data inappropriately or at least questionably. Have students examine the visual aids to determine:

- whether there is enough information presented in the visual
- whether the information is relevant
- whether the visual presentation is consistent (For example, if there are two graphs, check the axes to see if the scales are the same.)
- whether the information is appropriate for a visual presentation

ANALYZING ARGUMENTS IN VISUAL MEDIA (PAGE 82)

Examples from advertising and politics underscore the subtle complexities of meaning achieved by the use of visual elements.

■ A distinction is made between persuasive advertising and argument. "Genuine argumentation, by contrast, seeks to clarify thought in an effort to address an issue or solve a problem; ideally, it aspires to truth" (85).

DESIGN AND COLOR

This section draws attention to design aspects: placement, symmetry, image, proportion, size, and style. Color associations are briefly mentioned, such as white being associated with purity.

Activity: Color Associations

Make a list of colors, and have the class brainstorm for adjectives they associate with those colors. For homework, have them find photographs that exemplify the use of these colors to evoke those associations.

ART AS VISUAL ARGUMENT

This section uses examples of political art, war propaganda, and political cartoons to discuss the ways in which artists participate in cultural dialectics through art.

Activity: Political Cartoons

Either bring or have students bring political cartoons to class to discuss the underlying claims and warrants and their effectiveness. One source of current political cartoons can be found online at http://cagle.slate.msn.com/politicalcartoons/.

Activity: Art Gallery Visit

Many campuses have a gallery in which student art is displayed. Take your students to visit your campus gallery to examine the visual arguments their fellow students have created.

INTEGRATING VISUAL ELEMENTS AND TEXT

This section discusses the layering effect of using visuals to enhance written argument.

ANALYZING ARGUMENTS IN ELECTRONIC MEDIA (PAGE 97)

THE INTERNET

- "Internet technologies help people form and maintain communities by providing a ready medium for communication, discussion, and debate" (98).

- "Two main concerns skeptics often cite in their criticism of online forums for public discourse: the questionable nature of much of the discussion that occurs online and the sheer volume of online discussions" (98). Does the Internet foster more public discourse?

WEB SITES

ONLINE VERSIONS OF PRINT ARGUMENTS

- Many news sources, for example, do not differ greatly between print and online versions.

- Hypertextual Web Sites—"*Hypertext* refers to the capacity to link documents through hyperlinks that a user clicks to move from one document to another" (99). This type of document is not necessarily arranged in a linear fashion, so there are infinite ways in which users can access the parts of such a document, which effectively allows the reader to organize the writer's argument.

- "Hypertext enables authors to decide on alternative ways of presenting claims, evidence, and warrants" and "to embed multimedia . . . to help support an argument" (103).

Activity: Reading the Web

To draw attention to how hypertextuality can change their reading, have students, either in pairs or alone, attend to the way in which they read on the Web. Ask them to spend 20–30 minutes reading on the Web. You can either assign a topic for them to find out about, ask them to access a specific site, or just allow them to read what they want. Have them note what they do as they read. Do they link from one site to another? Do they follow tangents that are interesting to them? Do they get lost? At the end, have them reflect on what they learned both from their reading during that time and about their reading habits in a hypertext environment.

Web sites often employ traditional design techniques and newer multimedia capabilities to make implicit arguments. Marshall McLuhan's name is evoked late in the chapter (see page 111), but his declaration that "the medium is the message" would be an interesting discussion starter at this point in the chapter.

Activity: Creating a Hypertext Argument

Most colleges and universities provide Web space for students. If your college provides easy access to the tools necessary for students to create a personal Web site, you can assign students to write an argument that includes embedded hyperlinks to take advantage of the hypertextual possibilities described in this section. Two alternatives to designing an actual Web page are for students to use the link function in a word processing program to link to the Web or to use a stand-alone program such as HyperStudio.

ONLINE DISCUSSION FORUMS

- Asynchronous discussions potentially allow more people to be involved in a discussion and more time for those people to formulate a reasoned response.

- "The matter of *ethos* can also be complicated in online forums. Generally, there is no way of knowing who participants really are, whether they have any legitimate knowledge or experience related to the topic at hand, and whether they are being honest about what they say" (108).

The issue of the anonymity that the Web provides can be a good topic of discussion.

- *"Synchronous* forums . . . differ from asynchronous forums in that participants post and read messages in 'real time.'" In synchronous forums, multiple people are all composing and submitting responses at once, so they "do not lend themselves to considered debate about complex issues that require participants to keep up with the conversations" (109).

- "If you engage in synchronous discussions, you will be more effective if you can keep your statements short but clear and if you an focus on one claim at a time. Similarly, offer clearly identifiable support for a claim that can be easily digested by other participants" (109).

You might consider together how this newer type of communication could change the face of argumentation.

Activity: Online Discussion

Many campuses provide online discussion tools. If you haven't tried one of these in your courses before, you might want to experiment with one. Some tools that might be available are Blackboard™, WebCT™, or e-mail listservs. If no such tool is available, you might try Nicenet, which is a free discussion tool available on the Web at www.nicenet.org.

If this is your first foray into online discussion, you can start slowly by posting one question and (here's the trick) requiring students to reply to the question once and then respond to at least one post of a classmate. Be sure they have read Chapter 4 of *The Informed Argument* so that they have at least been introduced to the tips for "netiquette." Realize that you, as the instructor, will likely have to intervene to some extent to prod students to participate and think further. Even if you start small, chances are you will quickly find more and more uses for this tool.

RADIO AND TELEVISION

Very little of what appears on television is "genuine argumentation," and it is imperative that we are able to "distinguish between the many kinds of persuasion on television and the few genuine arguments appearing in that medium" (111).

IMPORTANT FEATURES THAT ARE SHARED BY BOTH RADIO AND TELEVISION (110–111)

- reach—audiences can range from the local area to international consumers.

- immediacy—the lack of printed text "requires the speaker to adjust diction, style, and arrangement so that listeners can follow the argument easily. Long, complex sentences can be difficult for an audience to follow . . ."

- sound effects—music or other sounds "might influence how you think about the claim being made."

Another important concept to note with students is the function of TV and radio in shaping and influencing public opinion.

Activity: Kennedy and Nixon and the First Televised Debate

Today, we are accustomed to seeing everything—from the arrest of felons, to courtroom proceedings, to the collapse of the World Trade Center towers—live on TV. When Richard M. Nixon debated against John F. Kennedy on September 26, 1960, however, televising presidential debates was a new concept. The debate went poorly for Nixon, and although he had been favored to win against the upstart Kennedy, many believe that his poor television performance led to his defeat. Interestingly, people who watched the debate on TV thought that Nixon was easily defeated; those who heard it on radio considered Kennedy the loser.

Check with your school library to see if it carries a video copy of this important debate. You might also consider comparing this to current political debates.

Transparency

These are the best of times for the worst of people. And for the toxic idea at the core of all the most murderous ideologies of the modern age. That idea is that human nature is, if not a fiction, at least so watery and flimsy that it poses no serious impediment to evil political entities determined to treat people as malleable clay to be molded into creatures at once submissive and violent.

George F. Will in *Newsweek*

5 Constructing Arguments

This chapter shifts from a focus on the reading to writing argument. It knits together the ideas of the previous chapters with specific strategies for constructing sound rhetorical arguments. Because many teachers like to begin a writing course by having students write, this chapter may provide a good starting point for the course, as many of the concepts that are presented in great detail in the previous chapters are summarized here. Because it summarizes important ideas, this chapter could serve as an advance organizer that will provide students enough background to start writing early in the course. Students could use this chapter to begin writing and then go back and read the other chapters on rhetoric to help them build on and revise what they write early in the semester. An advantage to this approach is that it emphasizes the development of the writing processes.

POINTS TO NOTE

Arguing "effectively means understanding the specific factors involved in each case" (114):

1. the rhetorical situation (See Chapter 3.)
2. the goals for argument (See Chapter 1.)
3. the medium (See Chapter 4.)

MANAGING THE COMPOSING PROCESS (PAGE 114)

Students come to college writing courses with a wide variety of backgrounds in writing. Their preparation for how to write has come from far and wide, so it's generally best not to assume that their experience will prepare them to use one vocabulary about how to write. Define the terms you use to describe the business of writing.

The *composing process* or the plural *composing processes* are terms writers, teachers, and students use, but often, these terms are used differently by different people. We talk about these processes because, in one way or another, proficient writers go through these processes when they create a piece of writing, although probably less consciously or deliberately than students do. Defining these processes as thinking tools and helping students use them deliberately when they're needed will help them learn skills and strategies that will transfer to other writing situations.

- **Invention or Prewriting** is the activation of related knowledge. The reader portion of *The Informed Argument* assists students with this activation as it provides information related to the writing in its margins. This helps students see that prewriting for argument is not simply a matter of brainstorming but of the thoughtful knitting together of available information with one's own understanding of the topic to build an informed argument.

- **Structuring or Organizing** is the process of considering how ideas logically fit together. This also is the consideration of how to utilize traditional arrangements: classical, Rogerian, or logical.

- **Drafting** is the activation of expressive language. During drafting, the writer fully expresses the ideas that were generated through pre-writing in paragraph form according to a general organizational plan.

- **Revision** is the consideration and evaluation of word choice, logic, relevancy, and sufficiency.

- **Reflecting** is the development of the student writers' thinking about their writings' patterns of weaknesses and strengths so that they can manage the writing processes independently.

- **Editing** is proofreading for grammar, syntax, and mechanics. This stage necessarily comes last so that the writer doesn't take the time to polish language that might be discarded in the process of revision.

UNDERSTANDING COMPOSING AS INQUIRY

"By composing an argument, you are carefully exploring an issue, learning about that issue and about yourself and others as well" (115). This quote could serve well to begin a discussion on the purpose of this type of writing in academia and the world at large.

DEFINING YOUR TOPIC

"[I]t is important to distinguish between a subject and a *topic*" (115).

- A **subject** is a general umbrella term under which more specific ideas can be explored.

- A **topic** is far narrower and explores a specific issue within a subject.

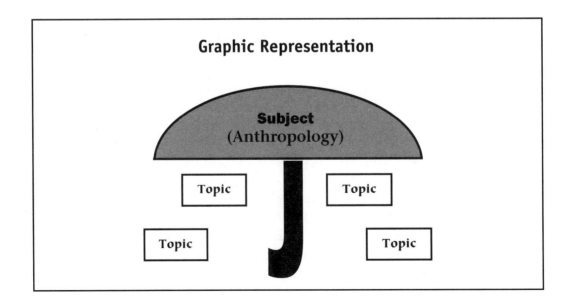

Activity: Matters of Opinion

Students have had a variety of experiences with the idea of opinion. Some students will have been taught that opinions should be kept completely out of their writing. Others have the idea that their opinions are more or less the only things that matter. Most (thankfully) have had more moderate experiences. If you foresee a problem with having students differentiate between personal preference and judgment, try this activity.

Have students form groups of three to four and give them six 3"× 5" cards. Give them about 15 minutes during which they are to make up four possible argument topics that are matters of judgment and two that they think are a matter of personal preference. If time is tight, you might provide a subject for them. Let them know that this is a game, so they should try not to be obvious. Ask them to write a topic in sentence form and NOT to label whether it is judgment or preference. Have them pass their cards to another group and have the other group evaluate the topics to see if they can tell if the issues are a matter of judgment or preference.

VARIATION: If your students are capable of easily discerning which topics are matters of opinion, you might have them brainstorm to support the topics that were generated by another group using the questions on page 116:

- Do I have an opinion about this topic? What is that opinion based on?

- On what grounds might anyone disagree with my opinion?

- Can I hope to persuade others to agree with my opinion?

- Can I support my opinion with evidence? (What types of evidence would I look for?)

"Almost all arguments involve *opinions*, but not all opinions lead to good arguments. . . . Be careful to distinguish between opinions that are a matter of taste and those that are a question of judgment. . . . Judgment involves logic. Our judgments are determined by our beliefs, which in turn grow out of basic principles to which we try to remain consistent" (116).

CONSIDERING AUDIENCE (refer also to Chapter 3)

IDENTIFYING YOUR AUDIENCE

- "Your understanding of your audience can help generate specific ideas for your argument and formulate those ideas in ways that may resonate with that audience. Moreover, if you approach argumentation as problem-solving, you will tend to see your audience not as an opponent but as a partner to your effort to address the issue at hand" (117–118).

- "As you develop your argument, assume that [some] readers will be skeptical. But don't dismiss their views; rather, consider their reasons for opposing your viewpoint and try to address their concerns as you build your own case" (118).

You may want to draw on the distinction made by Chaim Perelman in *The Realm of Rhetoric* (Notre Dame UP, 1982) between a particular audience and the universal audience (such as a teacher, members of the Film Society, or American college students). Perelman's universal audience is an imaginary construct consisting of "all those who are competent and reasonable . . . which may itself be made up for a variety of particular audiences." Students often do best when they direct their writing toward a particular audience, especially if it is one with whom they have some familiarity, such as college freshmen at their school. Some writers work best, however, when they envision a universal or idea audience, and, according to theorists such as Walter Ong, readers often play the role of audience they sense the writer has envisioned. When a writer seems to address us as reasonable people and members of a world community, we may, as readers, assume that role.

Activity: Prewriting

The sidebar "A Method for Exploring Your Ideas and Your Audience in Argument" on page 117 provides an excellent method for helping students prewrite. Prewriting too often becomes a kitschy activity that students try once or twice (because they're required to do so) and then abandon. However, spending time generating material with which to work is crucial for ensuring the quality of the support in the essay. To stress the importance of this type of thinking, consider using class time to do this and other prewriting activities.

MAKING CONCESSIONS

- "Identifying [others' valid] concerns enables you to understand the issue better and to construct an argument that may not only be more convincing but also more useful . . . In this way, you may bridge a gap between you and members of your audience who oppose your position, making it easier to reach a more substantial agreement . . . When making concessions, address what you think are your audience's most pressing concerns" (118).

Consider with your class the benefits of making concessions for those with whom we disagree.

UNDERSTANDING AUDIENCE EXPECTATIONS

Considering one's audience involves a fairly sophisticated ability to empathize. Good writing involves being able to imagine what words might sound like to another. It also involves being able to recognize one's assumptions brought to the writing.

- "Having a good sense of audience can also help you decide on examples and evidence that will best illustrate and support your claims" (119).

- Above all else, be truthful. "Never present anything to one audience that you would be compelled to deny to another" (119).

The Student example on pages 119–121 provides an excellent example of revision strategies aimed at targeting audience.

DEFINING YOUR TERMS

"Don't feel that you need to define every word you use, but you should define any important term that your audience might misunderstand" (124).

STRUCTURING AN ARGUMENT (PAGE 125)

This section details traditional ways in which students can arrange their arguments. Patterns of organizations are described here, but as noted in this chapter, these patterns are not mutually exclusive. Furthermore, real writing, and certainly the writing with which students are familiar, rarely follows rhetorical formulae exactly or exclusively. Real writing, good writing draws appropriately on all the available tools to convey its message.

The purpose of teaching writing is not simply to have students produce a product. When we teach students to write, we provide an opportunity for them to practice a way of thinking and communicating their learning. Help students see that thinking carefully about writing has larger implications for their learning and thinking in all subjects.

CLASSICAL ARRANGEMENT

The components of classical rhetoric are detailed in the sidebar on page 126.

- "Because classical theories of rhetoric developed at a time when most arguments were oral, the great works of classical rhetoric recommended strategies that could be easily understood by listeners" (126). This makes an interesting idea for class discussion. Now that we are a more visually-oriented society, does this style of rhetoric become less effective?

- "Classical arrangement can be especially useful when you feel strongly about an issue and you are trying to convince an audience to undertake a proposed course of action" (127). Again, this is a quote that could lend itself to becoming a conversation starter. Why does the arrangement work well in this situation?

ROGERIAN ARGUMENT (refer to Chapter 1)

- "Rogers focused on listening with understanding in order to avoid miscommunication that can too often accompany serious conflicts" (127).

- "A Rogerian argument may be most effective in situations in which people are deeply divided as a result of different values or perceptions" (128).

Rogers's thinking has wide implications for such a range of issues, but his thinking provides a ripe opportunity for discussing the links between rhetorical arrangement and audience.

A student example with an accompanying works cited page is provided on pages 129–132 to show how following the plan can yield a thorough and thoughtful essay.

LOGICAL ARRANGEMENTS

Inductive Reasoning (see Chapter 2) is "drawing a conclusion based on evidence you present" (132). Here are some considerations:

1. Try to arrange your evidence so that it leads your readers to the same conclusion you have reached.

2. Consider how specific kinds of evidence you have gathered will affect your readers.

3. Decide how much evidence is enough.

4. Interpret and analyze your evidence for your audience.

DEDUCTIVE REASONING

This reasoning "begins with a generalization [or premise] and works to a conclusion that follows from that generalization" (134). Note the Sidebar on page 134, "A Method for Reasoning Deductively," which suggests that writers work backward when planning a deductive argument to uncover the premise.

■ These are the steps for reasoning deductively (134–135):

1. Identify your conclusions. Make your conclusions #3 on your list.

2. Examining your reasons carefully. Make your list of reasons #2 on your list.

3. Formulate your premise. For this, "you need to establish the principle that supports [your] conclusion." "A premise can be a single sentence, a full paragraph, or more . . . The function of a premise is to establish a widely accepted value that even your opponents should be able to share" (135).

A student example is provided on pages 136–138.

USING THE TOULMIN MODEL

■ "The Toulmin model focuses on the claim you want to make—that is, the conclusion you are trying to reach or the assertion you hope to prove. Your task, simply put, is to state your claim clearly and offer persuasive reasons (what Toulmin called *data*) for that claim. The third element in the Toulmin system is the *warrant*, which is the assumption that connects the claim and the data" (138).

■ "The value of this model for constructing an argument lies in the way it requires you to articulate your claim precisely and to pay close attention to the adequacy of your reasons and your evidence without having to follow the rigid rules of formal logic" (139).

■ General advice on using Toulmin Model (139)

1. Try to articulate your central claim clearly.

2. "Before moving to your reasons for your claim, you should consider carefully whether that statement accurately represents the position you want to take."

3. "Brainstorm, listing the main reasons for your belief."

4. "Think about your warrant—the assumptions that lie behind the claim and connect your reason and claim."

5. "Develop specific evidence to support your claim and your reasons."

A student example with a references page is provided on pages 141–143.

- "What counts as good evidence will vary from one context to another" (144).

- "Your audience can affect not just the kind of evidence you use but also whether you need evidence for a particular point" (145).

This section points out questions to ask oneself while constructing argument. The list on page 145 would serve well as a checklist for peer response.

Activity: Peer Response

Providing numerous opportunities for students to consider how their writing affects others reinforces the idea that revision is an integral part of writing. Allowing class time for students to help each other with their writing can be rewarding in a number of ways. Student writers get to see how their peers go about writing, which is a form of modeling. It helps student writers become more accustomed to reading writing objectively, a skill which they often transfer to their own writing. And frankly, if peer response is learned well, the teacher's job becomes a bit easier, as students become better able to revise their own work after receiving constructive peer feedback.

WHAT MAKES FOR EFFECTIVE PEER RESPONSE?

1. Before setting students free to critique one another, have a discussion about what you see as the purpose of peer response. What are the benefits? What are the pitfalls? Have them establish rules for peer response.

2. Model an appropriate response. Use an anonymous essay from a former student (one whose author students won't be able to identify) and give copies to all students or put the essay on the overhead. Model what you would say to the writer, such as, "I like how you've done _____." "I'm a bit confused about _____."

3. You might want to teach peer responders to point out what has been done correctly and well rather than focusing on what isn't working.

4. Be specific in your charge to students. Be sure they have something specific and productive to do during peer response time. For example, have one session in which students help each other examine the writing for a clear thesis. Or have them answer the list of questions provided in the section titled "Supporting Claims and Presenting Evidence" or the list of questions on word use, both of which appear in Chapter 5.

5. You might want to have students bring additional copies of their papers so the authors can read aloud and have group members follow along and take notes.

6. Peer response is not simply time for proofreading. Of course, if students *really* revise, proofreading too early is a waste of time.

- "In constructing an effective argument, you should attend to how you employ the power of language—how you use diction, sentence structure, tone, rhythm, and figures of speech" (146). Many students will need these words defined for them.

- "As you work through your argument, think carefully about what kind of language will be most effective for the specific audience, rhetorical situation, and medium you are encountering" (146).

Teacher to Teacher

Appropriate word use presents a problem for many students. Eager to use academic language that they don't own or speak, some students write themselves into a proverbial corner. What they lack in vocabulary, they often try to make up for with a thesaurus, which leads to stilted or even incomprehensible prose. Convincing students to use less convoluted language is not always easy, but sometimes gently pointing out the difficulty you are having comprehending their writing and asking them to "say this in more words" or to "explain this differently" or to "let me hear your voice here" will help free them from the responsibility they feel to write in that pseudo-academic voice.

Part II: Working with Sources

6 Doing Research

Teacher to Teacher

Research is too often reduced to a meaningless exercise in cut and paste. Although there is no one "proper" way of going about research, I like to help students see research as a way of participating in a larger dialogue and as a method of knowledge construction rather than one for information regurgitation. Using the I-Search method developed by Ken Macrorie (*The I-Search Paper: Revised Edition of Searching Writing*. Boyton/Cook, 1988), students learn to

1. think about what they already know and can bring to the topic at hand;

2. pose specific questions they will seek to answer and that they really want to know the answers to;

3. search for information to answer the questions, making note of (a) what the information tells them and (b) how the new information relates to or changes their "big picture";

4. think about what they know about the topic once they're finished the process.

After going through the I-Search process, students have done the requisite thinking for writing a well-reasoned research paper. I find that revealing the larger, more philosophical purposes of research helps students approach research in a more thoughtful, engaged manner.

POINTS TO NOTE

When teaching *The Informed Argument*, emphasize that learning to work with sources is as important as learning how to argue. Point out that these two skills are closely related: The ability to find sources and read them critically makes it easier to argue effectively.

1. "*Primary research* requires firsthand experimentation or analysis."

2. "*Secondary research* involves investigating what other people have already published on a given subject" (152).

If your class is comprised mainly of freshmen and sophomores, you may need to help them understand the differences between the types of secondary sources they may use in college work. For example, first- and second-year students often have trouble understanding that the databases of scholarly articles they access through an Internet browser are not the same as Web sites. Few freshmen have learned about the existence of scholarly journals, so few quickly comprehend the difference between the popular press and scholarly work.

Most college libraries provide opportunities for classes to meet with a librarian to learn how to find resources in the library. In addition to the library tour, you might ask if a librarian would be willing to collaborate with you for another class period on the differences between the types of sources they have available through your library.

READING CRITICALLY (PAGE 152)

Critical reading requires students to read in an active and engaged way. This section details the underlying requisite skills required for active, engaged reading.

Readers often create their own texts by dwelling on some words and passing over others, and, of course, the words of almost any text can trigger responses shaped by personal experiences—responses which can either enrich a reading or lead to an interpretation that the text itself does not support. Supporting college students in their reading is essential.

PREVIEWING

Careful previewing (surveying) helps readers prepare to extract information from a text. Probably the most important benefit is that previewing helps the reader get an idea of the purpose and value of the reading, which tends to increase comprehension.

- Questions to answer while previewing (153–154)

  1. How long is this work?
  2. What can I learn from the title?
  3. Do I know anything about the author?
  4. What do I know about the publisher?
  5. Is there anything else I can discover by skimming through the material?

     —average paragraph length

     —special features

     —subtitles

     —abstracts

     —bibliography

ANNOTATING

This sidebar provides some tips on how to annotate simply to help a reader engage more effectively with a text.

- Methods for effective annotation (155)
    1. Use margins to define new works or identify unfamiliar allusions.
    2. Write comments.
    3. Jot down questions.
    4. Make cross-references.
    5. Write down your own response to an important point.

Teacher to Teacher

A book is a tool. Highlighting and annotating are enhancements that should help that tool become even more functional. College freshmen who have never had the opportunity to highlight a book often don't know what to highlight, so they highlight entire pages. When you assign this part of the book, you might try to help students understand that highlighting huge passages will require that they go back and read the entire passage again to find the point. Highlighting should just draw their attention to major ideas for easy reference.

Another helpful hint for many students is to use "sticky notes" to annotate a book or article. They can be used in a multitude of ways, from "think sheets" to flags for sections to refer back to.

SUMMARIZING

The ability to summarize undergirds one's ability to do just about anything else in academia. If a student can summarize what has been read, he or she can expand upon or critique ideas effectively. Summarizing, however, is not a simplistic exercise that is learned and abandoned in elementary school. As the level of difficulty of reading increases, so does the difficulty of appropriately condensing material to summary. Friend (R. Friend, "Teaching Summarization as a Content Area Reading Strategy," Dec. 2000/Jan. 2001 *Journal of Adolescent & Adult Literacy*) writes, "In order to enhance learning, summarization should be a process in which the ideas of a passage are related to one another, weighed, and condensed; a process of synthesis, not selection."

Activity: Summarizing Effectively

Focus on the skill of summarizing by having students write a number of summaries of increasingly complex materials.

SUMMARY WRITING STEPS (adapted from Friend's article)
1. Think of the passage as a whole.
2. Determine the author's thesis.

(Continued on page 40)

—What was the *whole* article about?

—What is the author's message about the topic?

3. Determine the central idea of each paragraph.

4. Check your work.

—Make sure it is one paragraph.

—Make sure your first sentence includes the thesis

—Make sure it is ALL your own words.

—Do not use the words *about, how,* or *the way.*

—Be sure nothing is repeated.

—Be sure it includes only a statement of the main ideas—edit out any details, examples, or anecdotes.

- "[A] good summary should indicate that the bias is part of the work in question. *But writers should not interject their own opinions into a summary of someone else's work.* The tone of a summary should be neutral" (157).

SYNTHESIZING

- "Synthesis requires identifying related material in two or more works and tying them smoothly together" (157).

- Questions to guide synthesizing (158)

    1. How does this material relate to whatever else I have already read on this topic?

    2. Does the second of two works offer support for the first or does it reflect an entirely different thesis?

    3. If the two sources share a similar position, do they arrive at a similar conclusion by entirely different means or do they overlap at any points?

    4. Would it be easier to compare the two works or to contrast them?

Two plans for presenting syntheses are provided on page 159.

TAKING NOTES (PAGE 159)

Many students' notes are incomprehensible to them. The idea of taking notes doesn't even occur to others. Take time to discuss this section.

- "Note taking refers to keeping notes on all your sources, ideas, and information for a single essay or project" (160).

Methods for taking and storing notes are detailed.

- "The important point to keep in mind is that you must give credit to the ideas of others, as well as to their words, when you are using sources in your writing" (161).

- *"Remember to put quoted material within quotation marks"* (163).

Teacher to Teacher

Despite the many cautions we offer, students often continue to plagiarize. What I see in our Writing Center are students who try to integrate the ideas of others but do so sloppily and without proper citation. Often, student writers plagiarize inadvertently because they don't understand how properly citing a work is different from co-opting the ideas within that work. Other times, they plagiarize because their reading level is not sufficient to effectively paraphrase the idea in the first place. It is worth your time to help students understand these distinctions and the skills to demonstrate them.

FINDING RELEVANT MATERIAL (PAGE 161)

The companion Web site for this text can be found by visiting http://www.english.wadsworth.com/yagelski/. On this site, you will find a page to aid students in finding appropriate sources. It provides access to the INFOTRAC database as well as direct links to many of the news sources used in the research for this text.

- Be flexible. "Although you may have a tentative thesis in mind when you being your search, it's often a good idea to delay formulating your final thesis until your research is complete" (164).

- "Your own research may ultimately support a belief that you already hold, but if you proceed as if you are genuinely trying to solve a problem or answer a question, your research may deepen your understanding of the issue and lead you to realize that you were previously misinformed . . . Ultimately, your argument will be stronger if you recognize that disagreement about your topic exists and then demonstrate why you favor one position over another—or show how different positions can be reconciled" (164).

USING THE INTERNET

- "When searching the Internet, you must carefully evaluate the material you locate—and recognize that his material can range from first-rate scholarship to utter trash" (165).

- "Not every scholar chooses to make completed work available electronically, so you can miss important material if you try to do all your research on the Internet" (167).

Use the page titled "Evaluating Web Resources" on Cornell University Library's Web site at http://campusgw.library.cornell.edu/t/help/res_strategy/evaluating/evaluate.html to provide your students vocabulary with which to discuss strengths and weaknesses of Web sites. After introducing this vocabulary, have them visit Widener University's Wolfgram Memorial Library's site that contains checklists for evaluating sites at http://www2.widener.edu/Wolfgram-Memorial-Library/webevaluation/webeval.htm. Have students visit examples of sites and evaluate them at http://www2.widener.edu/Wolfgram-Memorial-Library/webevaluation/examples.htm. Follow up their evaluations with a written reflection or an oral reporting of their observations to the class.

Teacher to Teacher

We all need to know where information comes from that we are consuming. Here's a little tidbit that might be of help to you in teaching how to determine the origin of a Web site. Web sites are just computer files. Perhaps you have made a sub-folder in your "My Documents" folder on your computer. Likewise, Web sites are composed of folders within folders, as indicated by the slashes in a Web address. It is often possible to "back up" a Web address to find out where it is coming from by removing the additional filenames and looking at the "root" of the address. So, for example, if you go to the Web site http://www.publicagenda.org/issues/nation_divided_detail.cfm?issue_type=americas_global_role&list=1 and you want to know more about the origin of the information, remove all but the first part of the URL, which is called the domain name. In this case, the original site is http://www.publicagenda.org/. If you end up somewhere that doesn't look like it is really the origin, it might just be a host. Another way to back up is to start at the end of the URL and remove one sub-filename at a time (the characters that appear between the slash [/] marks).

Take a look at the articles that appear on the Web sites below, and be sure to take a peek at the root site on which they are housed. I have students look at this type of site to see for themselves how they are likely to find information that is presented by people or organizations with skewed perspectives or are presenting information in an attempt to sell goods or services.

- http://www.virusmyth.net/aids/data/kmreason.htm from http://www.virusmyth.net

- http://www.ncpa.org/ba/ba230.html from http://www.ncpa.org

- http://www.jeremiahproject.com/smoke/et9803.html from http://www.jeremiahproject.com

- http://www.innernet.net/doco/sjo/add_treatment.htm from http://www.innernet.net/doco/index.html

SEARCHING FOR MAGAZINE AND JOURNAL ARTICLES

This section details ways to find magazine and journal articles. Of course, each college or university library subscribes to different databases, so you might find it helpful to contact your library to find out which databases are available for your use. On the Web site for this text, access to the INFOTRAC database (http://www.infotrac-college.com) is available with the key that is provided with the students' text.

SEARCHING FOR NEWSPAPER ARTICLES

This section recommends using *Lexis-Nexis*, which is the most comprehensive tool available for news articles.

USING ABSTRACTING SERVICES

- "Because it can be hard to tell from a title whether an article will be useful, abstracts offer an advantage over simple bibliographical citations. The summary provided by an abstracting service can help you decide whether you want to read the entire article" (173).

LOOKING FOR BOOKS

- Books "often represent the final and most prestigious result of someone else's research . . . Much of the best information you can find appears somewhere in a book, and you should not assume that your research subject is so new or so specialized that your library will not have books on it" (173–174).

- Check the catalog listing for basic clues about the book's usefulness for you:
  - the date of publication
  - the length of the book
  - the reputation of the publisher (175)

CONDUCTING INTERVIEWS AND SURVEYS (PAGE 175)

Tips for Interviewing (175–176)

- Evaluate the credibility of anyone you interview.

- Plan ahead for your interviews.

- Ask good questions.

- Be flexible.

- Consider using a tape recorder.

- Record the date of the interview and the full name and credentials or position of the person you interviewed.

Even those who are not statistics experts can conduct surveys. Here are some tips for conducting surveys (176–177):

- Carefully compose a list of relevant questions.

- Decide whether you want to administer the survey orally or distribute it in a written form.

- Decide how many people you will need to survey to have a credible sample of the population that concerns you.

- Consider whether it would be useful to analyze your results in terms of such differences as gender, race, age, income, or religion.

- Take steps to protect the privacy of your respondents.

Activity: Designing a Survey

Doing original research is labor intensive, but it provides students with a chance to participate in the generation of knowledge and a feeling of accomplishment. To reduce the burden of data collection on your students, consider having the class design one survey that all students can draw from when writing their subsequent arguments. Constructing the survey as a large group will also allow you to discuss and refine the questions they pose as part of a class so that you can have a measure of quality control.

7 Documenting Your Sources

COMPILING A PRELIMINARY BIBLIOGRAPHY (PAGE 180)

Anyone who has written a research paper of any substantial length understands the value of keeping track of source information. (Who among us has not had to run back to a library or search frantically in Infotrac for a source for which we *thought* we had written information down?) Students who are writing a lengthy paper for the first time won't realize how valuable finding a method for keeping track of bibliographic information will be in the long run. Take some time in class to talk with them about some ways of keeping track of the sources they use and about the long-term benefits of keeping track of sources. Even if students think they are only doing one-shot research on a topic, having carefully stored notes on their research may come in handy for them at some point.

Information stored using a bibliographic database program such as *EndNote* can be accessed by key word. It also formats stored information on the Reference or Works Cited pages for the writer.

If *Endnote* isn't available, students might consider keeping a research notebook that contains the information that such a program would help them collect. I provide a research form for my students such as the one below to help them keep track of the information they need.

Author:	
Editor or author of whole work:	
Title of article and page numbers or title of individual page from larger Web site:	
Title of publication (journal/newspaper/ book/Web site):	
Date of publication:	
Date of retrieval from Web:	
Additional information:	
Evaluate the source. Is it worth using? Does it specifically meet your needs? Is it on an appropriate academic level? How do you know it is? You may need to choose another if your answer is negative.	

ORGANIZING A RESEARCH PAPER (PAGE 180)

Outlining is explained here as a tool to help the student writer stay on track; however, outlining can be a mixed blessing. For some students, outlining can be inhibiting, as they see the outline as a fixed entity. Have students think carefully about how they use outlines or other organizational methods such as mapping or listing, and stress the idea that "you can rewrite an outline much more easily than you can rewrite a paper, so be prepared to rework any outline that does not help you to write better" (181).

INTEGRATING SOURCE MATERIAL INTO YOUR PAPER (PAGE 181)

- "Make sure that any quotations you use fit smoothly into your essay as a whole" (181).

- "Quote only what you need most, and edit long quotations whenever possible" (182).

- "Sources do not need to be quoted in order to be cited" (182).

CITING SOURCES (PAGE 182)

- "In general, you must provide documentation for
  - any direct quotation.
  - any idea that has come from someone else's work.
  - any fact or statistic that is not widely known" (183).

This is always a sticking point for students. What is common knowledge? There is no clear-cut answer to this question. My best answer to this is "when in doubt, cite it."

- There are three main styles of citation: MLA, APA, and Chicago. While others exist, these are the most common.

Teacher to Teacher

Teacher to Teacher: Students come to college having been taught a number of citation styles. High school teachers are less likely to stay abreast of changes in documentation than college instructors, but it is most likely counterproductive to deride their former teachers for not keeping up with these changes. You might want to explain that one major reason that they've learned different rules has to do with the advent of the Web and the resulting changes in documentation styles. Explain why you choose to use the style you are requiring of them and show them the current manual of style.

- Although the formatting of styles varies, "the purpose of all these systems is the same: to provide appropriate information about your sources" (183).

- "Notice that the same basic information is provided, no matter which documentation system is used" (184). The format of the information used reflects what the organization values.

FOOTNOTES AND CONTENT NOTES

- "Both MLA and APA recommend that writers use parenthetical, or in-text citations . . . ; traditional footnotes are not used for documenting sources. Instead, number notes are reserved for additional explanation or discussion that is important but cannot be included within the actual text without a loss of focus " (184).

PARENTHETICAL (OR IN-TEXT) DOCUMENTATION (PAGE 185)

- "*MLA style* . . . emphasizes the author and author's work and places less emphasis on the date of publication."

- "The author's last name is followed by a page reference, but do not repeat information that is already stated in the preceding sentence." (Examples are provided.)

- "*APA style* emphasizes the author and date of the publication."

- Identify the author of the work and the year in which the work was published; where appropriate, include page numbers preceded by the abbreviation "p." or "pp." It is not necessary to repeat any information that has already been provided directly in the sentence. (Examples are provided.)

ORGANIZING A BIBLIOGRAPHY

The *basic* organization is the same for APA and MLA. See pages 192, 193, and 200–203 for diagrams that are excellent visual aids for explaining the bibliographic forms.

Activity: Comparing APA and MLA

One way of teaching these is to make a comparison contrast chart on the board and have students consider the differences.

APA	Same	MLA
Use author's last name, first INITIAL.		Use author's last name, first NAME.
Date follows name. Place date in parentheses.		Date goes with publication information.
Capitalize only the first word of any title or subtitle.		Capitalize every important word in titles of books, articles, and journals.
Italicize titles of books, journals, magazines, and newspapers.		Underline or italicize the titles of books, articles, and journals.
Do NOT place quotation marks around titles of articles or chapters and do NOT italicize or underline them.		Place the titles of articles, stories, and poems in quotation marks.
	Alphabetize.	
	Indent the second and any subsequent lines one-half inch (or five spaces).	

Particularly helpful are the Checklist for Documentation on page 207 and Checklist for Manuscript Form on page 208. You might consider using these for peer editing guides when students have completed their final drafts and are preparing to turn in a final draft.

Part III: Negotiating Differences

Introduction to Reader

The readings in Part III are organized around six main themes, each of which is further divided into three sub-themes, or "clusters." This organizing scheme emanates from our view that arguments following familiar pro/con patterns tend to oversimplify important issues and thus work against problem solving. Accordingly, we have resisted presenting examples of arguments that fall easily into pro or con categories. Although each cluster of readings can stand on its own, the three clusters in each chapter are closely related; moreover, most clusters provide three or four perspectives on the topic at hand, rather than two "pro" arguments and two "con" arguments. We believe this organizing scheme will help students appreciate the complexity of the issues addressed in each chapter and offer instructors many more options for grouping readings and fitting the selections easily into their courses.

The themes of these six chapters reflect traditional issues—education, the environment, free enterprise, and so on—that are being transformed by recent social, political, cultural, and technological developments. The writers represent a range of interests, professions, perspectives, and cultural backgrounds. Moreover, the majority of readings are recent, reflecting contemporary points of view; they also reflect a diversity of media: there are selections from traditional print publications, such as the *New York Times*, newer publications such as *Z Magazine*, and online journals. Some classic arguments, such as Martin Luther King, Jr.'s "Letter from a Birmingham Jail," have been retained from previous editions, which helps provide historical context for contemporary arguments and also gives students traditional examples of argumentation.

WHAT YOU WILL FIND IN THIS PART

This part of the Instructor's Manual provides you with a range of resources for your teaching:

- pared-down summaries of the clusters and the individual readings for quick reference

- notes labeled "Teacher to Teacher" to help you see the rationale for including the reading in the chapter, as well as the intended purposes of the questions

- at least one additional discussion question for each reading (Many of these questions lean toward discussions of the topic at hand rather than toward rhetorical strategies. They are meant to help continue or enrich a class discussion and help students explore their own stances on issues.)

- an additional writing prompt is included for each cluster to provide an alternative to the "Negotiating Differences" prompt

- a list of suggested readings that you might use in addition to or instead of the readings provided in the chapter

Reading actively and critically are skills that many students seem to lack upon entrance to college. Because one's reading comprehension is intimately tied to writing in so many ways, it is imperative to help students develop their reading skills. Most students who are eligible for admission to your college can be fairly easily taught the necessary skills. If you encounter a problem with your students' reading skills, think carefully about what may be causing the problem. (You might also seek assistance from the learning assistance professionals on your campus, if you have a learning center.) I have found a number of reasons why students seem to have reading difficulties:

- Some students are assigned more difficult reading material in college than they have ever attempted to read before. High schools do not always use materials that help students develop a college-ready reading fluency. Reading skills, like writing skills, need to continually develop.

- Many students simply fail to realize the expectations their instructors hold, such as the assumption that thorough reading should be finished *prior to* the discussion or lecture period. Assigning written homework to be turned in prior to the discussion can help encourage students' class preparation.

- Many lack an effective method for annotating or note-taking while reading. For this reason, I teach students how to keep a reading journal, which is often a revelatory experience for students.

- Many have been conditioned to explore the upper reaches of critical thinking about a piece prior to ensuring that their basic comprehension of the writing is solid. In other words, students often form strong opinions about articles, but they blatantly misconstrue the message of the article. For this reason, I maintain that teaching summarizing and paraphrasing is key.

Students often feel very uncomfortable about revealing reading difficulties they experience, so it is important for the instructor to reassure them by creating an atmosphere in which they can learn these skills free from stigma. For example, I often introduce my lesson on summarizing by talking about the fact that although many of them last practiced summarizing in the fifth grade, the ability to summarize more advanced reading materials is a much more complex skill that requires more practice to master.

Consider assigning a reading journal that students can bring to class to refer to during class discussion. In addition to or instead of answering the discussion questions in the chapters, you could have them respond to a list of careful reading questions. You might want to have students create such a list for themselves, or you could provide them the list below.

Questions for Careful Reading

1. Summarize the content of the argument. Be sure you can put the main ideas of the argument in your own words.

2. Identify the areas of the text that are the most difficult and paraphrase the ideas you think the author is expressing—entirely in your own words.

3. Consider the context of the argument. At what time and under what circumstances was this piece written? Can you draw any inferences about this piece by considering the other arguments that address this same topic?

4. Find examples of the author's bias in the reading.

5. Make note of how this experience changes your understanding of "the big picture."

8 Ownership

Cluster 1: Who Owns Words and Ideas?

Despite the difficulty of legally defining ownership of intellectual property, the fact that we live in a culture based on private property often means that we have to try to determine the ownership of intellectual property. The authors of the essays in this cluster all address this need as it emerges in schools and in commercial culture. They examine questions of ownership of words and ideas in ways that may help you appreciate the complexity of intellectual property and consider the many interests that people have in trying to determine who owns words and ideas. As a group, these essays also raise a broader question about intellectual property: Is it really possible for anyone to "own" words or ideas?

Reading 1

Mathews, Jay. "Standing up for the Power of Learning." 2002. READING LEVEL 11.9.

Column about changes in honor code at Georgia Tech that had prohibited any collaboration between students. Companion piece to earlier column, "Shaping the Learning Curve." Argues for a position on cheating that tries to hold students accountable for doing their own work but at the same time acknowledges the reality that learning is often not an exclusively individual activity.

Teacher to Teacher

The questions for this cluster will elicit a range of responses, most of which require students to use personal experience. The only question that requires a specific response is number two, which asks the students to refer to "Appraising Evidence." This question asks your students to assess the use of personal experiences of students in the course as a basis for arguing against Georgia Tech's policy. Answering these questions will help students recognize the complexity of the issue.

ADDITIONAL DISCUSSION QUESTIONS

1. How do you learn best: in a group or alone? Does your ability to learn in a group change depending on the subject matter?

2. Should universities or professors be allowed to make non-collaboration policies? Who owns (or should own) an individual class and the rights to make classroom policies?

Reading 2

Kaminer, Wendy. "Heavy Lifting." 2003. READING LEVEL 10.7.

Focuses on the Stephen Ambrose plagiarism case. Argues that "Plagiarism is a kind of identity theft." Essay raises questions about what plagiarism is and to what extent writers can really create original texts.

Teacher to Teacher

Kaminer blasts Stephen Ambrose for plagiarism on ethical grounds that may not seem quite as dire to students. The questions that accompany the article provide an opportunity to help students really comprehend her position and explore the ramifications of her stance.

ADDITIONAL DISCUSSION QUESTIONS

1. Supporters of Ambrose think that Ambrose's omission of quotation marks should not lead to such severe charges. Detractors, many of whom are academics, say that such an act could not possibly be a mistake. Kaminer sides with the latter group, noting that, "this defense of Ambrose simply underscores his underlying offense: He doesn't author books, it seems, so much as he assembles them, relying on an army of researchers and other, less prominent historians." In this passage, Kaminer, in addition to raising the complex issue of authorship in today's publishing world, seems to be offended by Ambrose's lack of original thought. Ambrose had assistants who did the bulk of his work for him. Had Ambrose followed the rules to avoid plagiarism and simply used the ideas of lesser known historians, would his work have been acceptable?

2. Ideas cannot stay new for very long. When does an idea pass from an individual into the larger consciousness or discourse, making the idea part of a culture? How can someone claim the right to own an idea? For how long should and for what purpose can that right exist?

3. Copyrights protect creative pursuits, and without them, artists argue that they would not be able to make a living from their work. Kaminer takes the issue a step further than the financial losses artists suffer and says that because creative work "is self-expression (for people who think and write with some originality). Plagiarism is a kind of identity theft." How do you respond to this statement? Explain which reason for avoiding plagiarism is more compelling to you: that it protects the artists financially or that it protects them from identity theft.

Reading 3

Caplan, Ralph. "What's Yours?" 1998. READING LEVEL 10.0.

Caplan, an architectural designer, considers how we can determine when someone "owns" an idea. Caplan helps us see that arguments about intellectual property are not limited to words, music, or images. He suggests that arguments about intellectual property are really about the fundamental value of fairness and about how we wish to share our ideas and our abilities with one another.

ADDITIONAL DISCUSSION QUESTIONS

1. Does Caplan's tone in this article change or does it remain even throughout?

2. Caplan uses several literary references to make his points. Near the end of the article, he writes,
    "But Leavitt was writing fiction, in which personal experience may be transferable. In Charles
    Williams's *Descent into Hell*, Pauline tells Peter about a recurring event that terrifies her. He can't
    do anything about the recurring event, but he offers to carry the fear for her, just as he would carry
    a parcel or her books. It's still her fear, he explains, but with him as designated schlepper, she
    won't have to do the fearing." How does this example fit here, and how does it help him make
    his point about ownership?

3. How does the placement of the example of the Judith Langer lecture affect Caplan's argument?

Reading 4

Gillespie, Nick. "'Let's Roll': You Can Trademark Words but Not Meaning." 2002. READING
LEVEL 12.0.

*In this editorial, Gillespie argues that the use of September 11 hero Todd Beamer's phrase "Let's roll" for
commercial purposes is fairly inappropriate. He calls for people to remember the origin of the phrase.*

ADDITIONAL DISCUSSION QUESTION

• Claiming the right to use words exclusively by trademarking them is typically done in our society
   for reasons markedly different than is the case for the Beamer Foundation. What is your opinion
   about the trademarking and subsequent permissioning of the term "Let's roll"? What does
   Gillespie appear to think about this practice?

Explore Internet sites that sell term papers, such as *Cheat House* or *School Sucks* and consider the underlying premises by which such companies stand. As a specific response to this type of site, such companies as *TurnItIn.com* have sprung up to provide support to institutions by helping determine whether students are cheating. Take a look at *TurnItIn* and read their rationale for providing their product. Write a letter to the editor of your school newspaper in which you address the use of both of these kinds of technologies. This might be a good use of argument for inquiry.

ADDITIONAL SUGGESTED READINGS

Burnside, Julian. "Obscene Words." *The Vocabula Review* 4 July 2002. 9 July 2003 <http://www. vocabula.com/VRJULY02BurnsideALD.htm>.
   Offbeat and funny argument that calls into question our collective squeamishness about the word fuck.

Mathews, Jay. "Shaping the Learning Curve through a Code." *Washington Post*, April 16, 2002 9 July 2003 <http://www.washingtonpost.com/wp-dyn/articles/A58274-2002Apr16.html>.
   Interesting column about an honor code in a computer science course at Georgia State that prohibits collaboration between students. Raises some interesting issues regarding the nature of learning, cheating, and who owns knowledge.

Newitz, Annalee. "Buffy: Hero for the Columbine Generation." *Bad Subjects* July 16, 1999. 9 July 2003 <http://www.eserver.org/bs/editors/1999-7-16.html>.
   Argues against the censoring of TV shows aimed at children that too closely mimic real-life violence on the grounds that such shows are really exposés about how adults control ideas.

Orwell, George. "Politics and the English Language."

Roeper, Richard. "Garbage or Garb, It's All Protected Speech." *Chicago Tribune* 17 January 2001: 11.
   Interesting and short piece that uses a number of examples of people arrested for wearing "obscene" T-shirts to argue in favor of protecting such free speech.

Cluster 2: Who Owns the Body?

The essays in this cluster examine the complexities associated with our often astonishing capabilities to learn about, manipulate, and use our bodies through genetics and fertility science. They all ask different versions of the same question, *Who owns our bodies?* And they challenge us to think more broadly about what can be owned and by whom.

Reading 1

Rapp, Rayna, and Faye Ginsburg. "Standing at the Crossroads of Genetic Testing: New Eugenics, Disability Consciousness, and Women's Work." 2002. READING LEVEL 12.0.
   Well-reasoned argument intended to complicate the public discussions about prenatal testing for birth defects.

Teacher to Teacher

Because of its length and complexity, this article is accompanied by four questions that focus on student comprehension. This topic is likely an unfamiliar one to most students, so taking time to answer all four of the comprehension questions will be important. This might well be done in small groups to aid students in accomplishing this task. Questions five and six help students focus on Rapp and Ginsburg's rhetorical strategies.

ADDITIONAL DISCUSSION QUESTIONS

1. Why do Rapp and Ginsburg show the relationship between genetic testing and consumer health issues? Is this an effective detail in this article?

2. Examine how Rapp and Ginsburg link women's work, changes in societal structure, genetic engineering, and disability consciousness. Are these links strong enough to warrant those affected by these issues to participate in setting research agendas?

Reading 2

Freely, Maureen. "Designer Babies and Other Fairy Tales." 2002. READING LEVEL 8.8.

Points out that fertility science presents people with very complex choices to make. Argues that the many different kinds of arguments made about such situations complicate the already difficult decisions facing parents and others. Sorts through the many different voices in debates about reproductive medicine and asks us to focus on how the issues are being debated.

Teacher to Teacher

This article is, in effect, a meta-argument, as it points to the problems of the larger discourse on fertility science. To understand the article requires that students understand the writer's rhetorical position. The questions for this article ask students to both comprehend the article's content and analyze Freely's rhetorical strategy. Although the reading level is low, students may find that comprehending the significance of Freely's reasoning requires careful reading and reflection.

ADDITIONAL DISCUSSION QUESTIONS

1. Freely lays out a list of very large concerns that people have had about reproductive science. She acknowledges all these concerns as "important questions" and goes on to define reproductive science as representative of societal change. Is casting the argument in these terms an effective tactic for persuading her readers to see her point?

2. Freely examines the rights she has over her own reproductive rights and declares that laws regarding reproductive technology should allow women the same types of rights over their bodies. How are the rights to contraception and technologically-assisted birth the same or different from one another? Who should be allowed to choose what those rights should be?

3. How does Freely's argument present the concept of eugenics? What are the connotations of the word *eugenics* in this article?

Reading 3

Henig, Robin Marantz. "Adapting to Our Own Engineering" 2002. READING LEVEL 12.0

Many people worry about unforeseen consequences of human cloning, and moral arguments are often made against cloning as well. But some proponents argue that research into cloning can lead to beneficial medical advances. Henig has monitored these debates and likens them to other advances in fertility science that once caused great concern but now seem commonplace.

Teacher to Teacher

The first question here asks students to state their comprehension. The rest of the questions help them analyze and evaluate Henig's writing style and choices. Students would likely be able to answer these on their own and could follow up with a class discussion or debate.

ADDITIONAL DISCUSSION QUESTIONS

1. What is your position on in-vitro fertilization and cloning? What reasons do you have for feeling this way about these technologies?

2. Which types of reasons should take precedence in determining whether these technologies are right or wrong?

Reading 4

McElroy, Wendy. "Victims from Birth." 2002. READING LEVEL 9.6.

Discusses an unusual case involving two women who used reproductive techniques to make it more likely that the child they would have would be deaf, just like the two of them. She argues that the choice should have been his. She asks us to consider who owns our physical identities in an age when medical science makes it possible to determine and alter those identities.

Teacher to Teacher

This is an easy read that is likely to elicit strong responses from students. What will be important here is to focus first on how McElroy makes her point. The questions will help students analyze McElroy's premises and her use of evidence to support her claims. This would make an excellent piece on which to hold a class debate.

1. Is there a difference between deaf lesbians seeking a deaf sperm donor and two heterosexual deaf people choosing to have children?

2. McElroy notes that McCullough "Pass[es] over the problem of equating race with a genetic defect" when she says that "Black people have hard lives" but that they wouldn't have experienced such criticism had they chosen a black sperm donor. Consider how this equation could be seen as problematic and how it could be seen as reasonable.

ALTERNATIVE WRITING ACTIVITY

Consider how several of the authors in this cluster have brought up—either implicitly or explicitly—the idea of eugenics. *Eugenics* is a term for the study of methods of improving genetic qualities by selective breeding. Those who support eugenics have proposed such policies as the forced sterilization of the poor. Search your library to learn about eugenics and consider for yourself whether fertility science has returned to the promotion of this idea.

ADDITIONAL SUGGESTED READINGS

Annas, G. J. "Rules for Research on Human Genetic Variation—Lessons from Iceland." *New England Journal of Medicine* 342 (15 June 2000).

Bailey, Ronald. "To Enhance or Not to Enhance?" *Reason Online* 8 May 2002. 9 July 2003 <http://www.reason.com/rb/rb050802.shtml>.
Straightforward argument in favor of responsible genetic engineering to avoid birth defects.

Gulcher, J. R. and K. Stefánsson, "The Icelandic Healthcare Database and Informed Consent." *New England Journal of Medicine* 342 (15 June 2000).

Krauthammer, Charles. "Cloning Debate is Not Another Monkey Trial." *Town Hall* 10 May 2002. The Heritage Foundation. 9 July 2003 <http://www.townhall.com/columnists/charleskrauthammer/ck20020510.shtml>.
Lively argument against cloning for research purposes on the grounds it is "the ultimate commodification of the human embryo."

Saletan, William. "Fetal Positions." *Mother Jones* May/June 1998.
Thoughtful, reasoned argument in favor of cloning for medical research. Argues against applying the terms of the abortion debate to arguments about cloning.

Teichman, Jenny. "Bottle Babies." *Quadrant* 45(9) (Sept. 2001) 32-34.
Considers ethics of permissive policies toward artificial insemination and in vitro fertilization. Author is clearly against these practices.

Cluster 3: Who Owns Music?

Issues of copyright law, profit, censorship, and identity are all ways that ownership and control of music surface in public discourse. The various kinds of questions about the ownership of music raised by the essays in this cluster reflect important social, legal, economic, and even moral concerns that affect all of us, regardless of our musical tastes.

Reading 1

Ian, Janis. "Free Downloads Play Sweet Music." 2002. READING LEVEL 8.9.

Lively and interesting argument in favor of free music downloads on the Internet by a well-known and accomplished musician. Ian believes that musicians and consumers can all benefit from free music downloads; moreover, she thinks free downloads are good for the art itself by making music more widely available.

T e a c h e r   t o   T e a c h e r

Questions for this article help students analyze Ian's strategies for making her point. This article provides an interesting contrast to the ones regarding intellectual property in the first cluster.

ADDITIONAL DISCUSSION QUESTIONS

1. Ian raises the point that industry-run focus groups are problematic ways to gather information. Such groups are used to make many decisions that affect the public. What are some pros and cons you can think of having to do with industry-financed market research?

2. What do you think is the record industry's motive for trying to do away with MP3 sharing technologies? Do you think Ian is correct in saying that MP3 sharing is more likely to boost than destroy sales?

3. Near the end of her article, Ian points to a list of problems that the recording industry has: "there are arguably only four record labels left in America (Sony, AOL Time Warner, Universal, BMG—and where is the RICO act when we need it?), when entire genres are glorifying the gangster mentality and losing their biggest voices to violence, when executives change positions as often as Zsa Zsa Gabor changed clothes, and 'A&R' has become a euphemism for 'Absent & Redundant' . . ." What is the benefit of pointing to these issues? In your opinion, why are they more, less, or equally important issues? How does identifying gangster rap as a problem limit Ian's intended audience? How is this a risky rhetorical choice?

Reading 2

Taruskin, Richard. "Music Dangers and the Case for Control." 2001. READING LEVEL 12.0.

Argues for some exercise of control of music to serve the public good. Music, like other kinds of art, isn't just a form of artistic expression for Taruskin, but a means of conveying ideas as well. Contends that governments routinely try to control the distribution of certain ideas—with good reason. Many Americans will likely disagree.

T e a c h e r   t o   T e a c h e r

This article presents an idea that will be very foreign to many students—that classical music can be political. All the questions help students examine his rhetoric, but many of the questions are also offered in an attempt to have students connect their own experiences to the issues Taruskin confronts.

---

1. In what ways does Taruskin's description of other cultures' attitudes toward music establish his biases?

2. By examining his examples of how people over the ages have misused music, explain what you think Taruskin believes to be the purpose of music.

3. Taruskin writes, "But who takes art more seriously? Those who want it left alone or those who want to regulate it? Moreover, the laissez-faire position entails some serious denials. Some say that art is inherently uplifting (if it is really art). Others say that art is inherently transgressive (if it is really art). The words in parentheses, designed to discourage counterexamples and make refutation impossible, merely empty the statements of real meaning. Does such a defense really show a commitment to the value of art or merely an unwillingness to think about it?" In this paragraph, he addresses those on both sides of the debate and uses rhetorical questions to indicate the direction he wants to take the argument. Is this an effective paragraph?

4. As a musicologist, Taruskin reads music as many of the rest of us read words on a page. Is his reading of Adams's composition an effective way of making his case?

5. At the end of his article, Taruskin makes the claim that although he deplores censorship, forbearance is necessary. Has he adequately established that these two things are necessarily different from one another? How (and why) do you think art should be (or not be) controlled?

Reading 3

Ogbar, Jeffrey O.G. and Vijay Prashad. "Black is Back." 2000. READING LEVEL 12.0.

Worries about who owns or controls the meaning of rap and hip-hop music. If these musical styles are, as they believe, forms of cultural expression that give voice to the concerns of Blacks, especially Black youth, then the commercialization of rap and hip-hop and its popularity among mainstream groups amount to the theft of Black identity as expressed in that music.

Teacher to Teacher

This article will likely resonate with students, so the higher reading level may pose less difficulty for less proficient readers. But it will probably still be important to ensure that students have understood the more complex academic language that the authors use. The questions provide some checks for comprehension but focus mostly on rhetorical strategy.

1. Paraphrase the last sentences of Ogbar and Prashad's article: "Hip-hop alone cannot rise up to the task of political transformation—this is pop culture not a manifesto. However, by looking at the particular political situations and aspirations of its musicians, we can trace its rise as an iconic power and its demise when the assimilationist powers of the capitalist economy flatten out the music's richness to render it a message of personal gain." These complicated sentences reveal their main concerns about hip-hop's effects on culture around the world.

2. Consider the idea of the necessity of forbearance Taruskin expressed in his essay. In what ways do Ogbar and Prashad's thinking here suggest a similar thesis? How does the major idea here differ from Taruskin's?

3. Given what you know about hip-hop music, do you think that style of music is more or less political than Ogbar and Prashad explain here? Are there more ways to categorize hip-hop music than the ways in which the authors do here? Do the ways in which music is categorized matter? Does music really influence people's behavior?

4. Is American rap music too culturally specific to share with people in other countries? Could it be detrimental to people in Malaysia or South Africa?

5. Having the right to express oneself through music in the United States is largely held as a right. If music permeates culture and changes people's outlook and lifestyle—for the better or worse—should it be censored?

Reading 4

Toomey, Jenny. "Empire of the Air." 2002. READING LEVEL 12.0.

Presents the corporate ownership of large numbers of radio stations across the country as cause for concern because the similarity of stations reflects a concentration of control of the radio airwaves in the U.S. Believes such control placed in the hands of a few companies gives those companies too much control over what we hear on the radio. Argues that radio is not just a business but a public asset.

Teacher to Teacher

The questions for this reading focus mainly on rhetorical strategy. Question two is an important comprehension and evaluation question that will likely provide a good springboard for small group discussion. As question five points out, this article contains syllogistic reasoning, making this a more complex reading assignment.

ADDITIONAL DISCUSSION QUESTIONS

1. Toomey and the Future of Music Coalition see the deregulation and the incipient consolidation of the ownership of radio as an affront to, among others, musicians. To whom do you think she is addressing her argument?

2. The premise of Toomey's argument is that radio is a community resource that is being misused, and she is making a call to action for people to get involved with restoring that resource. What are other arguments against deregulation that could be made about this issue?

3. Who should control the airwaves if the government owns them?

4. United States business practices do not allow for monopoly—the practice of one entity controlling a single market. With evidence pointing to a dwindling number of entities that control the radio market, what are the business ethics to be considered in the consolidation of radio station ownership?

Write an argument to inquire in which you consider your own position on digital copying of music, censorship, cultural aspects of music, or ownership of radio stations.

ADDITIONAL SUGGESTED READINGS

Megalogenis, George. "Don't Ban Eminem, Give Him an Oscar." *The Australian* 24 April 2001: 9.
Interesting argument against censoring offensive rap lyrics. Argues that music lyrics should be treated in the same way that film is treated with respect to ratings and censorship.

Mitchinson, Paul. "How Dare You Strike That Chord!" *Andante* June 2002. 9 July 2003 <http://www.andante.com/article/article.cfm?id=17438>.
Very intriguing argument against criticism of classical music on ideological grounds. Nice example of Rogerian argument as well.

9 Education

Cluster 1: What Should Be Taught in Schools?

To make an argument about what to teach students is to make a statement about what you believe education is—or should be—for. If Dewey was right that education is ultimately about democracy, then one question to be answered is, *What kind of democracy do we want?* And there is rarely unanimous agreement between Americans about how to answer that question. As you read the following essays, think about how you might answer that question. These writers make arguments about specific issues or ideas that should be taught in American classrooms, but their arguments all rest on beliefs—implied or explicitly stated—about the kind of society we want our schools to help us build.

Reading 1

Just, Richard. "Enroll: Why Berkeley Students Should Punish a Teacher by Taking His Class." 2002. READING LEVEL 12.0.

Asserts that a controversy at UC Berkeley prompted debate about whether or not a college course should be overtly political. (Raised questions about the role of politics in teaching and learning in American colleges and universities.) Reveals that this old debate is as timely as ever. Drawing on personal college experiences, asks us to think about what should happen in college courses—and to what end.

Teacher to Teacher

Questions provided with this reading address comprehension and assist in the analysis of writing strategies. This is an essay that is likely to elicit strong responses from students, so it would make a good piece for class discussion.

ADDITIONAL DISCUSSION QUESTIONS

1. Do personal politics have a place in the classroom? In which classroom?

2. Does allowing opposing viewpoints to be openly debated strengthen classes?

3. Just notes that he preferred to have his professors announce their political biases on the first day of class when he was in college. Think about a class in which you have no idea about your professor's politics. How would learning this information change your relationship with that professor? Would if affect your learning in that class? Does it depend on the subject?

4. Was Shingavi's move to exclude people who held views contrary to his own from his course acceptable? Give some reasons for your answer.

Reading 2

Kurtz, Stanley. "Balancing the Academy." 2002. READING LEVEL 12.0.

Ideas have great power because they affect how people understand the world around them and influence the decisions people make as they interact with one another. Article asserts that the political nature of ideas that come from our colleges and universities is why we should pay attention to what American scholars say and write. Supports the efforts of people who keep watch over the apparent political content of college courses. Takes up the controversy surrounding campus-watch.org to argue that students and others must find means of challenging what author believes is a left-wing ideology on campuses.

Teacher to Teacher

This reading allows for a good discussion regarding ethos. Questions in the chapter provide ample opportunity for students to establish comprehension of this complex writing.

ADDITIONAL DISCUSSION QUESTIONS

1. Kurtz writes, "In South Asian Studies, for example, scholars who had nothing at all to say about politics or foreign policy were branded as bigoted and neo-colonial 'Orientalists,' simply for studying religious ritual or family psychology. The very practice of scholarship outside of Said's leftist political framework was considered to be a subtle form of imperialism. For example, by writing about Hinduism, or by dissecting the dynamics of Indian family life, scholars were said to be turning Asians into "exotic" foreigners—with the subtle implication that such strange and irrational creatures deserved to be deprived of the right to self-rule." How should we learn about other cultures? Explain some reasons why each of these perspectives, Kurtz's and Said's, could be correct.

2. Kurtz writes, "The best way to challenge anti-American bias within the academy would be to do so in scholarly venues." How do the conflicts that arise among scholars affect the rest of society? How do they affect students? Are these conflicts important to know about? Should they be handled "in scholarly venues," the popular press, or somewhere else?

3. Kurtz writes, "My only concern is that a substantial number of scholars who take issue with the post-colonialists—scholars who see things more along the lines of Bernard Lewis, Ernest Gellner, and the rest (yes, and even Dan Pipes!)—be allowed back into the academy. My hope is that someday, the argument with Said's followers that today can play out only on the Web site of Campus Watch might someday be readmitted to the academy itself."

4. Kurtz raises the point that younger conservatives who disagree with the older "tenured radicals" in academia are barred from gaining employment opportunities. Tenure is a tradition in the field of academia. After a trial period, a professor who gains tenured status is given protection from summary dismissal. The tradition of tenure has long been debated in the academy. In addition to Kurtz's concern, what are reasons you can see for and against tenure?

Reading 3

hooks, bell.* "Toward a Radical Feminist Pedagogy." 1989.

Argues for a kind of education that is both collaborative and confrontational, one that intentionally challenges convention.

Teacher to Teacher

hooks's ideas are likely to resonate with many students, but they will not be familiar ideas. This reading should be accompanied by class or small group discussions to help students understand it. Questions provided for this reading allow students to comprehend the reading by connecting it to their own experiences.

ADDITIONAL DISCUSSION QUESTIONS

1. hooks begins with assumptions that become more apparent as the reader delves into her argument. Which of hooks's assumptions do you recognize in this piece?

2. Have you experienced teaching that connects personal experience to learning in the classroom? How did you feel about that learning experience?

3. What is the opposite view to that of hooks? How would that view likely be argued?

Reading 4

Takaki, Ronald. "An Educated and Culturally Literate Person Must Study America's Multicultural Reality." 1989. READING LEVEL 12.0.

Argues for the importance of requiring multicultural education. Suggests the purpose of such requirements is to help students understand diversity in order to live and work together.

Teacher to Teacher

The topic of this reading may be unfamiliar to readers, but they do have relevant personal experience that can inform their reading of this piece. Use the questions provided to help them comprehend and analyze the writing. Spending some time drawing out students' personal experiences with attempts at multicultural education will likely help even the more reticent readers connect with the topic.

ADDITIONAL DISCUSSION QUESTIONS

1. Have you, personally, had any experiences that relate to the type of multicultural education Takaki recommends? Have you taken such a course? Have you felt the need for one at your school?

---

*bell hooks does not capitalize her name in print.

2. Takaki is very specific about how multiculturalism should be taught. Does this specificity strengthen or weaken his argument?

ALTERNATIVE WRITING ACTIVITY

In response to one essay in this cluster, write an essay that clearly identifies what you believe is the purpose of education. The central question you should seek to answer is "What should be taught in schools?"

ADDITIONAL SUGGESTED READINGS

Banner, James M., Jr. "Teaching About Religion." *Basic Education* 47, Oct. 2002. 9 July 2003 <http://www.c-b-e.org/be/iss0210/a2banner.htm>.

Berlak, Harold. "Standards and the Control of Knowledge." *The Nation* 13 (Spring 1999).

Fisher, George. "Power Over Principle." *New York Times* 7 September 2002: Opinion-editorial page.
Argues that military recruiters should not have been allowed at Harvard Law School—or any law school—because the military's policy about gays violates important principles that law schools should uphold.

Hicks, Jerral. "Morality in Public Schools: What to Teach and Not to Teach." *The Challenge of the New Millennium.* New Falcon Press: 1997 <http://www.innerself.com/>.
Listing of the specific moral values Hicks believes should be taught in schools. Argues that "cross-cultural morals do exist."

Hirsch, Jr., E. D. "Why Core Knowledge Promotes Social Justice." *Common Knowledge* 12.4 (Fall 1999) <http://www.coreknowledge.org/>.
Succinct statement of Hirsch's emphasis on core knowledge as center of curriculum. Argues that such a curriculum promotes learning as well as social justice by teaching all kids the same things.

Just, Richard. "Keep Enrolling: In Defense of Politics in the Classroom." *The American Prospect Online* May 24, 2002 <http://www.prospect.org/>.
Follow-up to the earlier piece in which Just answers several critics who took issue with his argument.

Kurtz, Stanley. "Students Fight Back." *National Review* December 2, 2002 <http://www.nationalreview.com/>.
Addresses the controversy over the Web site noindictrination.org. Raises the larger question of academic freedom in useful ways. Also raises interesting questions about the Internet as a medium for protest.

Menands, Louis. "Undisciplined." *Wilson Quarterly* Autumn 2001 <http://wwics.si.edu/>.

Ohanian, Susan. "Standardized Schools" *The Nation* September 30, 1999 <http://www.thenation.com/>.

"One Nation Under God." *New York Times* June 27, 2002: Opinion-editorial page.
Argues that the appeals court ruling that found the Pledge of Allegiance unconstitutional is wrong.

Orr, David W. "The Liberal Arts, the Campus, and the Biosphere." *Ecological Literacy* SUNY Press: 1992. 97–108.

Cluster 2: How Should We Determine What Our Children Learn?

The essays in this cluster address concerns about curriculum and assessment. The authors of these essays offer their views on testing and tracking more than 100 years after the Committee of Ten's famous report. But, in effect, these authors are doing the same thing that the Committee of Ten did: trying to come to terms with how best to educate and test students. Ultimately, then, these essays reveal that arguments about testing and tracking are really arguments about what education should be.

Reading 1

Martin, Eleanor. " 'No' is the Right Answer." 1999. READING LEVEL 10.1.

Essay by a high school student who refused to take the state-mandated tests in Massachusetts. Explains why she refused and makes a case against standardized tests like the MCAS. Although essay focuses on the required state tests in Massachusetts, argument addresses larger questions about standardized testing and student learning—questions that continue to stir up heated debate nationwide as more states implement their own high-stakes tests.

Teacher to Teacher

This is an easy essay to read and one that will likely interest most traditional-aged college students. Because of its accessibility, this is a good essay with which to elicit a lively and open class discussion.

ADDITIONAL DISCUSSION QUESTIONS

1. Martin asks, "How can four years of learning and growing be assessed by a single standardized test?" What has been your personal experience with standardized tests? Based on your experiences, do you think Martin's assertion here is accurate? What alternatives to standardized testing have you experienced?

2. Martin says that the "supposed rationale" of the MCAS test is "that students are not learning enough in school." This is a powerful indictment of this standardized test. Why do we have standardized testing?

3. Martin asks, "How can someone who has been speaking English for three years be expected to write essays with correct spelling and grammar, which is a requirement to receive a proficient score?" This raises the question of whether standards can be one-size-fits-all. Should education require exactly the same thing of all students? What are some arguments that Martin puts forth in this article that shows what her answer would likely be?

4. Martin argues, "If the MCAS test is instituted in Massachusetts, the scores will become a major consideration for parents when they choose a school for their children. Schools will therefore want their scores to be as high as possible. Programs such as Metco, which integrates inner-city students into suburban schools, may be discouraged since it has been shown that inner-city students do not score as well as suburban students." What are the underlying arguments that Martin makes here?

Reading 2

Williams, Patricia J. "Tests, Tracking, and Derailment." 2002. READING LEVEL 12.0.

Placing students into educational "tracks" is to match the curriculum to students' needs and abilities has always been controversial, in part because it isn't clear that special programs or "tracks" serve their intended purposes. Article asserts that tracking students—for whatever purpose—ultimately leads to more problems than it solves. Short argument takes a position against tracking on the grounds it prevents equality in education.

Teacher to Teacher

Williams's article employs a fairly intellectual vocabulary. It will be very important to ensure that students are not put off by this language. This topic is one that has touched all students in one way or another—either because they were tracked or because they experienced inclusive education. The questions provided focus mostly on rhetoric. You might consider having students paraphrase the sections of this article they consider difficult in order to check their comprehension. Also, prior to their reading this article, you might hold a general class discussion about the way their elementary or secondary schools were administered to help them with the ideas in this article.

ADDITIONAL DISCUSSION QUESTIONS

1. Williams makes some generalizations about spending and educational administrative decisions in the first paragraph of the article. How effective is the use of such generalizations in this argument?

2. Willams says that "A system that teaches only the sopranos because no parent wants their child to be less than a diva is a system driven by the shortsightedness of narcissism. I think we make a well-rounded society the same way we make the best music: through the harmonic combination of differently pitched, but uniformly well-trained voices." An underlying question here is *Who deserves to be taught?* Have you experienced a tracking system in your educational career? What effects did it produce on the students who experienced it?

3. Williams argues that "discussions of educational equality are skewed by conflation of behavioral problems with IQ, and learning disabilities with retardation." She goes on to point out that these issues are not the same thing and that all children need the same thing: "ordered, supportive environments." Considering your personal experience as a student, do you agree or disagree with the assertions Williams makes here?

4. How is Williams's argument similar to and different from Hirsch's?

Reading 3

Cizek, Gregory. "Unintended Consequences of High Stakes Testing." 2002. READING LEVEL 11.4.

Maintains that carefully constructed standardized tests are a crucial element in efforts to improve public education. Argues that high-stakes tests lead to a number of important and beneficial consequences for students, schools, and teachers alike.

ADDITIONAL DISCUSSION QUESTIONS

1. Using a common practice in academic writing, Cizek refers to a previous article he wrote to make a point in paragraph 10. How does this reference to his own writing affect your reading of this particular article? What do you think of this as a practice in writing?

2. Cizek notes that "most testing specialists—and most of the public—simply favor coming clean about the source and magnitude of the subjectivity, and trying to minimize it." Is it possible, or desirable, to minimize subjectivity in education?

3. "Education is one of the few (only?) professions for which advancement, status, compensation, longevity, and so on are not related to personal performance," claims Cizek. This is how he makes his case for the rationale for resistance against accountability. Do you agree or disagree with his point?

4. Consider the advantages that Cizek attributes to the proliferation of high-stakes tests. Which examples provide more compelling evidence of the advantages of the tests? Which ones are less compelling? Describe the effect of his arrangement.

Reading 4

Ollman, Bertell. "Why So Many Exams? A Marxist Response." 2002. READING LEVEL 12.0.

Asserts that, despite constant criticism of schools and calls for reform, public education in the U.S. effectively serves the basic economic system on which American society is based: capitalism. Believes the many problems typically associated with schools actually reflect the needs of capitalism rather than the needs of individual students.

1. What does Ollman mean when he uses the analogy of the liberal and the Marxist who see a beggar?

2. Describe what you perceive to be Ollman's underlying beliefs about the way teaching and learning should be undertaken.

3. As a Marxist, Ollman sees exams as training for future workers in a capitalistic society. He constructs a list of ways in which exams "teach" children to uphold the status quo. In what ways is this list persuasive, and in what ways is it a flawed argument?

4. At the end of this article, Ollman takes a wider view and points to the ways in which he sees economic trends driving conservative reform movements in education. In what ways does this risky rhetorical strategy prove effective, and in what ways does it appear weak?

ALTERNATIVE WRITING ACTIVITY

Knowing for sure whether students have learned what the teacher has taught is part art, part science, and part mystery. How do we know what students have *really* learned? Surely tests provide teachers and students with some gauge of student learning. What other ways can teachers assess student learning? Write a proposal for a method of assessing student learning that would work for you as a learner.

As another alternative, you might look into how your school admits its students. Admissions are typically based on assessments appraised by high school teachers (g.p.a.) and on aptitude tests such as the SAT or ACT. Other factors also play into admissions. The Supreme Court reviewed the University of Michigan's policies for admission in June 2003 because of the weight that school placed on race in the admissions process. Find out who at your school makes decisions on admitting students and on what basis. Write an essay in which you explore the principles upon which these decisions are based.

ADDITIONAL SUGGESTED READING

Bollinger, Lee. "Debate Over SAT Masks Perilous Trends in College Admissions." *The Chronicle Review* 12 July 2002 <http://chronicle.com/free/v48/i44/44b01101.htm>.
Bollinger argues that the real issue surrounding the SAT is the competition for admission to "brand-name" schools in higher education.

See www.noindoctrination.org and www.campus-watch.org: Both purport to be watchdogs keeping an eye on "politically correct" college professors.

Cluster 3: How Should We Pay for Education?

As schools struggle to pay for the education they provide, debates about education funding are likely to intensify. But ultimately these debates remain intense not only because the economics of schooling are often complicated and difficult, but also because Americans continue to believe, as Horace Mann did, that education is a public obligation.

Reading 1

Friedman, Milton. "The Market Can Transform Our Schools." 2002. READING LEVEL 12.0.

Asserts that the principles of the free market will ultimately lead to better schools. Believes in a child's right to education, but maintains it is the free market that will ensure that right to education. Good example of conventional, logical argument.

Teacher to Teacher

The questions in the chapter will help students monitor for comprehension and consider how Friedman developed his piece. Helping students see how Friedman weaves statements that reveal his politics throughout the piece will provide a good lesson in critical reading.

ADDITIONAL DISCUSSION QUESTIONS

1. What kind of schools would Friedman like to see?

2. Friedman draws an analogy between the use of school vouchers and food stamps. Consider what this argument presupposes.

3. Friedman notes that providing vouchers the same way the G.I. bill was implemented after WWII would be most effective. What reasons can you think of to agree or disagree with this argument?

4. Friedman, an economist, writes, "The market will respond as fully and rapidly to the increased demand for private schools generated by the expansion of vouchers for elementary and secondary education. Private voucher programs, financed by foundations and individuals, plus the limited government programs so far enacted have already brought forth a market response." How does his use of an economic argument affect you as a reader?

5. Friedman writes, "School vouchers can push elementary and secondary education out of the nineteenth century and into the twenty-first by introducing market competition on a broad scale, just as competition has made progress possible in every other area of economic and civic life." In what way do you interpret this statement?

6. Consider the views of Michael Apple that appear in the complication box. How do the views of Friedman and Apple come into conflict?

Reading 2

Sowell, Thomas. "Flagging Flagships." 2002. READING LEVEL 12.0.

Points out that even state universities, which have traditionally been funded with public money, pay less and less of their costs with tax dollars. Proclaims that as universities stray from their traditional mission, the taxpayer is increasingly being asked to fund activities, such as research, that are not central to the educational mission of the state university. Implicitly raises questions about what the mission of higher education really is—and who should pay for it.

Teacher to Teacher

Although college students attend college, they aren't necessarily familiar with the ways in which their schools are funded or with the multiple functions the institution might serve. Indeed, many students don't understand that university professors are usually required to produce research in their field. Take some time to talk about the different types of schools there are, starting from what they know about their own college or university. The questions will help them explore Sowell's argument, but they will need to gain a basic understanding of the alternate purposes of universities if they are to fully comprehend this reading.

ADDITIONAL DISCUSSION QUESTIONS

1. What experiences have you had at colleges or universities that help you understand Sowell's argument?

2. In your own view, what is reason why states sponsor institutions of higher education?

Reading 3

Stark, Andrew. "Pizza Hut, Domino's, and the Public Schools." 2001. READING LEVEL 12.0.

Well-reasoned essay that examines the issue of commercialization in public schools. Argues that some deals between schools and corporations actually benefit students.

Teacher to Teacher

This is a lengthy but very interesting essay that employs sophisticated reasoning to arrive at its conclusions. The author of the textbook points to this as an example of Rogerian argument. Because this issue is one that can lead students to fascinating thinking about a range of subjects—the responsibility of schools, school funding, the ethics of advertising to children, etc.—it will likely be worthwhile to spend the time necessary to help your students make their way through it.

ADDITIONAL DISCUSSION QUESTIONS

1. How many paragraphs of Stark's essay would you consider to be his introduction? When are you sure you know where his own argument begins? Is this an effective writing strategy?

2. Stark notes that *Channel One* can't be accused of reducing the quality of its programming because it doesn't have to draw viewership since students are a "captive audience." Do you agree with his argument? If you have seen *Channel One* programming, do you remember the quality of the content? Was it less than, equal to, or better than other news to which you were being exposed?

3. One fundamental discussion that underlies this argument is whether or not television should be used as a teaching tool. What have been your personal experiences with television being used in the classroom?

4. Stark thinks the conflict of interest in using a corporation's curriculum or materials is only a "mild" conflict of interest. What is your reaction to this?

5. Do programs such as Campbell's Labels for Education influence your family's decisions to purchase or not purchase a specific item?

6. Is the Pizza Hut reading program subject to the same argument Stark makes about *Channel One*? Is a reading program that provides goods from a public company the same as bringing content into the classroom? Is the difference significant?

7. Define the words *commercialism* and *consumerism*. How are they similar, and how do they differ?

8. Do you see a difference between the Scholastic book fair program and *Channel One*?

Reading 4

Sheehan, John. "Why I Said No to Coca-Cola." 1999. READING LEVEL 9.8.

> *Short and very interesting essay by a Colorado school board member who cast the lone vote against a proposal to have his school district sign a marketing agreement with Coca-Cola.*

Teacher to Teacher

This is a less daunting piece of reading than the one by Stark. It doesn't provide the kind of extended reasoning that the Stark piece does, but it does provide a well-thought-out argument. The questions provided help students consider their own opinions on the topic and consider how the author crafted his writing.

ADDITIONAL DISCUSSION QUESTIONS

1. Is advertising to students in classrooms a breech of trust?

2. Sheehan notes that raising money by allowing corporate advertising in schools is letting the state's legislature "off the hook" for providing necessary funding for schools. Why do you agree or disagree with this assertion?

3. Sheehan ends by looking toward the future, raising the worry that the deal with Coca-Cola will lead to more and more deals that bring advertising to students. Is this an effective tactic?

ALTERNATIVE WRITING ACTIVITY

One way that colleges and universities save money is to reduce the number of full-time faculty they employ by hiring part-time or "adjunct" faculty and graduate students to teach classes. Although many of these instructors are excellent, these teachers sometimes have fewer credentials and less experience than full-time faculty, and they are usually responsible for large sections of introductory courses. These teachers are often paid very little for their work and most do not receive benefits such as health insurance. Read about the issues facing adjunct faculty online at http://AdjunctNation.com. After becoming informed about this issue, write an essay in which you take a position on the trend toward relying on part-time faculty in higher education.

ADDITIONAL SUGGESTED READINGS

Miner, Barbara. "Keeping Public Schools Public: Tuition Tax Credits: Vouchers in Disguise." *Rethinking Schools Online* Winter 2002/2003 <http://www.rethinkingschools.org/archive/17_02/Tax172.shtml>.

Rauch, Jonathan. "Reversing White Flight." *Atlantic Monthly* October 2002: 32.
Well-written and persuasive argument in favor of school vouchers on the grounds that they would help revitalize poor neighborhoods. Draws on the work of economist Thomas Nechyba to support the claim.

10 Environments

Cluster 1: What Is Common Ground?

The essays in this cluster address questions of community. How do we compare "incommensurables"? How do we decide what's best for *all* of us, even if it means that our decisions will not be good for *some* of us? What is the common good? And how should we use our common ground?

Reading 1

Will, George. "In Defense of Hallowed Ground." 2002. READING LEVEL 11.0.

> *Will believes that when we preserve historic American battlefields, we preserve our nation's collective memory as well. For Will, the hallowed ground of such battlefields is an important part of our identity as Americans. And that belief provides a twist to the typical arguments about whether to preserve special places like battlefields or to develop them for our economic benefit. Makes a case against building residential housing and corporate offices on the site of one of the great Civil War battles at Chancellorsville, Virginia.*

Teacher to Teacher

The questions provided with this easy-to-read article help students carefully consider Will's premises. Especially because of its reference to the hotly contested issue of the World Trade Center monument, the article is likely to elicit divided opinions from students, which could provide a good opportunity for class or online discussion.

ADDITIONAL DISCUSSION QUESTIONS

1. What are the premises on which Will rests his argument? Do you agree or disagree with them?

2. How effective is the likening of the attack on the World Trade Center to the way a "brat kicks a beehive"?

Reading 2

D'Souza, Radha. "Global Commons: But Where Is the Community?" READING LEVEL 12.0.

> *The rapid growth of international trade seemed to break down national borders and challenge traditional ideas about community and citizenship. For many people, the idea of "the commons" no longer seemed connected exclusively to local places or cultures; instead, the earth itself seemed to become our commons. Expresses deep reservations about the development of this idea of a global commons. Traces the idea of the commons in India and reveals that different cultures have different ways of understanding what constitutes common ground. Challenges us to think carefully about what we really mean by "the common good" in a changing and diverse world.*

ADDITIONAL DISCUSSION QUESTIONS

1. Do you agree with D'Souza's statement that "Capitalism destroyed communities bound to time and place, tied to history and geography"?

2. Discuss what she means by saying that she is a product "of colonisation."

3. How does your own cultural heritage influence your views about the common good?

Reading 3

Bollier, David. "Rediscovery of the Commons: Managing for the Common Good, Not Just for the Corporate Good." 2002. READING LEVEL 12.0.

Journalistic argument that there are some things—property, resources, even ideas—that neither governments nor businesses have an exclusive right to; there are some things that belong to everyone. The difficult question is, What are those things? Argues against a market-driven view of the commons; contends it has become the dominant way of thinking about the common interest. Instead proposes a more sweeping vision of a commons in which "ecological stability, social values, aesthetic concerns, and democratic traditions should carry as much weight around the policymaking table as economic analysis."

ADDITIONAL DISCUSSION QUESTIONS

1. Think of some examples of social commons in which you participate. How could the ways in which these communities are formed and managed be applied to a larger segment of the population?

2. How have you seen evidence of the movement toward "the commons" that Bollier claims is emerging?

3. As Bollier asks us in the article, "compare diversity of expression on TV or radio with that of the Internet." Do you agree that the existence of this diversity is evidence of the emergence of a new commons?

Reading 4

Sunstein, Cass. "The Daily We: Is the Internet Really a Blessing for Democracy?" 2001. READING LEVEL 12.0.

Suggests that despite the power of new media—specifically, the Internet—to inform and connect, we lack a true public sphere in which "a wide range of speakers have access to a diverse public." The Internet has the potential to be part of that public sphere, the article asserts, for most Americans it has become a means for accessing only the information that interests them. As a result, it is not a forum for confronting the diversity of views on which a healthy democracy depends. Well-documented argument rests on a particular vision of what a democracy should be.

Teacher to Teacher

Although it is long and complex, this is a fascinating article that will likely interest students with its discussion of how the familiar technologies impact politics and culture. The questions help students review the content to check their comprehension. Depending on how you intend to use this cluster, you might consider just choosing a few that focus on one or two issues for students to answer.

ADDITIONAL DISCUSSION QUESTIONS

1. What do you think is the purpose of the Internet? How do you typically use it?

2. What role should media play in democracy?

3. How could the lack of public forums influence one's ability to read and understand argument?

4. Public Radio is touted for its depth in covering issues. Listen to the program "All Things Considered" on your local NPR affiliate station and compare it with the 11:00 news from your local channel. What are the pros and cons you can see to each style of reporting? (For information on how to find your local NPR station, go to npr.org.)

ALTERNATIVE WRITING ASSIGNMENT

Imagine you are on an advisory board for the use of a state park on the outskirts of your town. A number of people—hikers, campers, bird-watchers, and fishers—have issued complaints about the increasing use of the park by all-terrain vehicle users. There had been no rules written previously limiting the use of these vehicles in the park. Those complaining about the ATVs are angry over noise, air pollution, and the destruction of trails. In a group of at least three students, discuss the positions of both sides and try to find a solution that takes as many people's needs into consideration as possible.

ADDITIONAL SUGGESTED READING

Siegel, Fred. "The Death and Life of America's Cities." *The Public Interest* Summer 2002 <http: //www.thepublicinterest.com/>.

Cluster 2: How Do We Design Communities?

In a sense, all the essays in this cluster address the question of how we determine what kinds of communities we should have. Ostensibly, these essays are about the problems associated with the growth of our communities A few of the writers discuss "sprawl," while others describe the "smart growth" movement. Their essays remind us that when we argue about practical problems like sprawl, we are really addressing deeper—and often more difficult—questions about how we should live together.

Reading 1

Plotz, David. "A Suburb Grown Up and All Paved Over" 2002. READING LEVEL 9.7.

Journalist description of the controversy over a law prohibiting homeowners in Fairfax County, Virginia, one of the wealthiest counties in the country, from paving their yards. Traces the origins of the law to concerns about growth, development, and especially immigration—longstanding issues that have often caused conflict among Americans. Plotz raises questions about the social effects of economic development and prompts us to consider what kinds of communities we wish to have.

Teacher to Teacher

This reading is accessible and uses an example that will likely engage students' interest. Plotz highlights the interconnectedness of a range of issues that most people haven't considered collectively before. The questions help students connect their personal experience with Plotz's example and examine the argument's premises.

ADDITIONAL DISCUSSION QUESTIONS

1. Compare the neighborhood in which you live to the one Plotz describes. Do your experiences of living where you live help you to understand his argument, or do your experiences contradict his points?

2. Who should make decisions about what homeowners do with their property? On what do you base your argument?

Reading 2

Postrel, Virginia. "Misplacing the Blame for Our Troubles on 'Flat, Not Tall' Spaces" 1999. READING LEVEL 9.7

Argues that contemporary life requires trade-offs: our lifestyle choices have both positive and negative consequences. Addresses a much larger matter: What kinds of communities do we really wish to live in? Suggests that proponents of smart growth embrace a vision of community that differs from the lifestyle that many suburbanites consciously seek. Also suggests that "smart-growthers" wish to impose their vision on others.

ADDITIONAL DISCUSSION QUESTIONS

1. Examine your own concept of a perfect living community. Where do you live? Is that ideal to you? If it isn't ideal, explain how you would like it to be.

2. What "trade-offs" in lifestyle do you think are acceptable, and which ones would not be acceptable? For example, would you live in a townhouse to reduce energy costs? Would you build a house in an unpopulated rural area to avoid traffic?

3. Paraphrase the first sentence of Postrel's final paragraph: "The anti-sprawl campaign seeks to impose a static, uniform future through nostalgic appeals to an idealized past."

Reading 3

Meadows, Donella. "So What Can We Do—Really Do—About Sprawl?" 1999. READING LEVEL 8.9.

Demonstrates that sprawl is a public policy issue. An opponent of unchecked development refuses simply to criticize developers; refuses to reduce the problem of sprawl to a pro-con debate. Suggests we all benefit from municipal services and economic development, no matter how fervently we may support environmental protection. Essay is an effort to address a complex problem through understanding rather than by opposing those who disagree.

ADDITIONAL DISCUSSION QUESTIONS

1. From what you read in the paragraph describing St. Louis, discuss whether or not you'd like to live there and why. Now look at her description of Oslo. Would you like to live in a place like that? How does your reaction to these descriptions affect your reading?

2. What are Meadows's reasons for opposing sprawl?

Reading 4

Wilson, Robert. "Enough Snickering. Suburbia Is More Complicated and Varied Than We Think." 2000. READING LEVEL 12.0.

Argues that we need to understand suburbs in part because they reflect our values and our visions for the lives we wish to have. Explores not only what suburbs are, but also what they mean to our sense of self as Americans. Reveals that although not a big fan of the way suburbs have evolved since the early twentieth century, also sees suburbs as an important part of American culture.

Teacher to Teacher

Because it was originally published in an architectural journal, this essay makes a number of references that students probably will not readily recognize—such as "the Garden City movement" or to architectural icons such as Frank Lloyd Wright. Take some time prior to their reading the article to examine the marginalia to help them comprehend the ideas more easily. The questions range from comprehension to analysis to evaluation.

ADDITIONAL DISCUSSION QUESTIONS

1. Do you agree that "Nothing can be less hip than suburbia"? What does this mean, exactly?

2. Wilson writes, "The biggest problem with suburbia is that we are all so certain that we know what it means. We watched *Father Knows Best* and read our Updike, and even a recent film like the Oscar-laden *American Beauty* confirms what we think we know: suburbia is a dull, sterile, unhappy place." Who is the "we" to whom he refers here?

ALTERNATIVE WRITING ACTIVITY

Examine the geography of the town in which you are living. How is it laid out? How would you characterize the areas of development: suburban, urban, rural? How do the ideas in the articles of this cluster relate to your town? What is good about the geographical layout? What could be improved upon? Do you identify any problems with the use of the land? What is likely to happen within the next ten years given the population and the housing available? Write a letter to the zoning board in which you make a proposal for changes you think should be implemented.

ADDITIONAL SUGGESTED READINGS

Turner, Wood. "Whose Land Is This Land?" *Common Dreams* July 9, 2002 <http://www.commondreams.org/views02/0710-09.htm>.

Wimsatt, William Upski. "The Fear Economy." *Adbusters.com* Spring 1998 <http://www.adbusters.org/magazine/21/fear.html>.

Cluster 3: What Is Our Relationship to Nature?

The essays in this section explore this connection between humans and the wilderness. In one way or another, these writers take up the challenge of defining our relationship to wilderness. The loss of wilderness areas raises questions about their value to us. Is their value only a function of the economic benefit they might produce—such as the lumber from the trees that are removed from a wilderness area when it is developed? Or does the value of wilderness lie in something more than profit, as Thoreau believed?

Reading 1

Carson, Rachel. "The Obligation to Endure." 1962. READING LEVEL 12.0.

Values espoused regarding the natural world—values that deeply influenced a generation of environmental advocates—emerge subtly but powerfully in a discussion of the physical and biological effects of chemicals in the environment.

Teacher to Teacher

This piece is accessible for most students and an important one to assign if you decide to deal with the topic of the environment. Many will have read this in high school. The questions will allow students to look at how the piece was argued and how it fits into the larger dialogue on the natural environment.

ADDITIONAL DISCUSSION QUESTIONS

1. Near the end of the essay, Carson writes in the first person. What is the effect of this technique?

2. Carson writes, "Have we fallen into a mesmerized state that makes us accept as inevitable that which is inferior or detrimental, as though having lost the will or the vision to demand that which is good?" How do you respond to that question?

Reading 2

Bailey, Ronald. "Silent Spring at 40." 2002. READING LEVEL 12.0

Argues that Carson played fast and loose with scientific facts in making her argument against pesticide use in Silent Spring. *Offers a detailed and extensive examination of those facts in an effort to call Carson's argument into question. Reminds us that any text can be understood as an argument—and that even science relies on argument and rhetoric.*

Teacher to Teacher

Bailey's article may come as a surprise to many students. The questions provided will allow students to read the text carefully and the marginalia will help them understand how it fits into the larger dialectic.

1. Examine your ethical response to this argument. In your opinion, if DDT is known to decimate bird populations, is that sufficient evidence to ban the substance?

2. Is the evidence that Bailey provides sufficient for you to believe that it is a reasonable argument?

3. What effect do you think Bailey's argument would have on an audience of people who consider themselves environmentalists? On an audience of those who consider themselves civil libertarians?

Reading 3

Turner, Jack. "In Wildness Is the Preservation of the World." 1996. READING LEVEL 12.0.

Suggests that neither those who seek to preserve wilderness areas nor those who oppose such preservation understand the wild. Contends that our wilderness is packaged and managed in parks and preserves that are more like museums than genuine wild areas. Advocates a sense of self as intimately part of the wild—in a very physical sense. Only direct experience of the wild—and this sense of ourselves as wild—will lead to the kind of passionate commitment to wilderness that Turner believes is essential for preserving wilderness.

Teacher to Teacher

This reading is from the Deep Ecology school of thought, which will be foreign to most students. The marginalia will come in handy in helping students understand that Turner is part of a larger movement of thinkers. The questions can guide students through a careful reading. You might want to spend some time helping them determine how they feel about these issues in addition.

1. Turner's argument may seem extreme at times, and you may wonder about the feasibility of the kind of direct experience of the wild that he advocates. Can everyone have such experience?

2. After identifying his claims and warrants, ask yourself whether *you* accept them. Have you ever read or heard claims and warrants about wilderness similar to Turner's? What is his line of reasoning similar to? What causes your personal reaction to Turner's ideas?

Reading 4

Shiva, Vandana. "Values Beyond Price." 1996. READING LEVEL 12.0.

Challenges those who care about the environment to rethink the relationship between humans, nature, culture, and commerce. Arguing that monetary values are at the root of the ecological crisis, pushes readers to understand environmental protection as something more than a conflict between economic development and wilderness preservation. Believes arguments about environmental protection cannot be separated from issues of social justice.

Teacher to Teacher

Shiva's reasoning is fascinating but will likely be unfamiliar to the majority of students. Most of the questions provided with the text are careful reading questions to really help them understand the implications of her thinking. As with all the pieces that introduce unfamiliar ways of thinking about issues, this piece may warrant a more extended class discussion.

ADDITIONAL DISCUSSION QUESTIONS

1. Are you convinced that there is an environmental crisis, as Shiva does? Read Bjorn Lomborg's essay (see Additional Suggested Readings) and compare their ideas.

2. How does Shiva's use of a female pronoun to describe nature affect your reading of this piece?

3. In your view, are poverty and social problems related to environmental destruction?

ALTERNATIVE WRITING ASSIGNMENT

You unexpectedly inherit 600 acres of land that is completely unspoiled. It is home to a variety of wildlife and indigenous plants. You can use it yourself, sell it, or donate it to a wilderness charity, such as the Audubon Society. Considering the ideas of the writers in this cluster, write an essay in which you explore the options you have available and make a decision about what to do with the land.

ADDITIONAL SUGGESTED READINGS

Global Climate Coalition: A Voice for Business in the Global Warming Debate. 2000. <http://www. globalclimate.org/>.

Lomborg, Bjorn. "The Skeptical Environmentalist Replies." *Scientific American* May 1, 2002 <http://www.sciam.com/article.cfm?articleID=000001E0-157B-1CD4-B4A8809EC588EEDF>.

Regis, Ed. "The Doomslayer." *Wired* February 1997 <http://www.wired.com/wired/archive/5.02/ ffsimon_pr.html>.

11 American National Identity

Cluster 1: Who Gets to Be an American?

What exactly does it mean to be an American? Who decides? And *how* should we decide who will become an American? The authors of the essays in this cluster all address these questions, sometimes focusing on policy and sometimes on ethnicity, race, gender, or national origin. In a sense, these authors all seek the same thing: immigration policies that contribute to a society that is consistent with American ideals.

Reading 1

Perez-Zeeb, Celia C. "By the Time I Get to Cucaracha." READING LEVEL 12.0.

Writer believes that concerns about immigration may have more to do with race and gender than with jobs and taxes. Focuses attention on the laws governing marriages between immigrants and American citizens and points out how those complicated laws place women at a disadvantage. Also examines the role that ethnic stereotypes about Hispanic people play in public debates about immigration.

> ## Teacher to Teacher
>
> This is a reading that will be of interest to most students because of its reference to a recognizable TV program. Because the article uses a familiar example, the questions focus more on rhetorical strategy than on comprehension.

ADDITIONAL DISCUSSION QUESTIONS

1. What is your own standpoint on the use of "ethnic" humor? Is it always, sometimes, or never appropriate?

2. Are you familiar with any examples of marriage between immigrants and American citizens as Perez-Zeeb describes them? How does your own experience inform your reading of this argument?

3. How effective is Perez-Zeeb's argument? Locate the points that were most effective for you and explain why they were effective. Locate the points that were least effective for you and explain why.

Reading 2

Brimelow, Peter. "A Nation of Immigrants." 1992. READING LEVEL 11.8.

Argument goes beyond policy issues to the complicated question of what constitutes a nation. Does it have to do with ethnic or racial identity? Or is it a matter of political borders and geographic location? Suggests such questions must be answered if there is to be acceptable resolution to the continuing conflicts regarding U.S. immigration policy.

Teacher to Teacher

This is a lengthy, academically-oriented piece. However, it provides important insight into the dialectic on immigration in the U.S. Questions are designed to assist students with careful reading.

ADDITIONAL DISCUSSION QUESTIONS

1. Why does Brimelow question the value of asserting that the U.S. is a nation of immigrants?

2. In paragraph 21, Brimelow alludes to the battle of Agincourt. When was this battle fought? Who won? And why was this outcome significant?

3. How effective is the comparison Brimelow makes between a speeded-up film of clouds and the development of American history?

4. How would you describe the tone of this article? Can you point to specific lines that support your view?

5. Paraphrase the difficult passage in paragraph 13: "Mass literacy, education, and mobility put a premium on the unifying effect of cultural and ethnic homogeneity."

Reading 3

Hornberger, Jacob G. "Keep the Borders Open." 2002. READING LEVEL 12.0.

Hornberger makes his argument in favor of an open immigration policy from his perspective as a libertarian.

Teacher to Teacher

The thinking here is fairly straightforward, so the questions focus more on rhetorical strategy. Use the marginalia to help students understand how Hornberger's political agenda is apparent in this essay.

ADDITIONAL DISCUSSION QUESTIONS

1. What does Hornberger mean by his comparison of the wall in California to the "ugliest wall in history"? Is this an effective comparison?

2. Hornberger's essay begins, "In times of crisis, it is sometimes wise and constructive for people to return to first principles." What are "the first principles" to which he refers? Will all readers necessarily have the same principles in mind when reading this?

Reading 4

Camarota, Steven. "Too Many: Looking Today's Immigration in the Face." 2002. READING LEVEL 12.0.

Camarota addresses the main issues that often emerge in debates about immigration: concerns about jobs, schools, taxes, and poverty. But in addressing those issues and providing extensive factual evidence, Camarota also presents a view of what he believes America should be.

T e a c h e r   t o   T e a c h e r

Use the marginalia to help students understand how Camarota and the American Immigration Law Foundation use statistics differently to prove opposing points. Questions help students understand how Camarota crafts his arguments and arrives at his conclusions.

ADDITIONAL DISCUSSION QUESTIONS

1. Think of examples of people you know who have immigrated to the U.S. How do your experiences inform your reading of this argument?

2. What is the America like that Camarota would like to see? Is this similar to or different from the way you would like this country to be?

3. Examine how Camarota makes the point that less diversity among immigrants is problematic. What do you think about this argument?

4. Compare Camarota's discussion of the acceptance of American history with paragraph 41 of "Letter from a Birmingham Jail" by Rev. Dr. Martin Luther King, Jr.

ALTERNATIVE WRITING ACTIVITY

The Melting Pot theory of American identity holds that those immigrants from foreign cultures, once they've arrived in this country, should blend to form a new, hybrid cultural mix. You might think of someone taking a pot full of crayons and melting them to create a whole new color. The Salad Bowl or Ethnic Stew theory holds that each person should maintain his or her own cultural traditions regardless of where the person lives. Go to the Internet and learn more about these ideas about immigration then write an argument in which you propose a system of how we should deal with immigration and cultural mixing in the U.S.

ADDITIONAL SUGGESTED READINGS

Gazer, Nathan, and Daniel Patrick Moynihan. *Beyond the Melting Pot.* Cambridge: The MIT Press, 2nd edition, 1970.

Jacoby, Tamar. "A Nation of Immigrants." *Wall Street Journal* April 29, 2002.
   Short essay that questions U.S. immigration policy in the wake of 9/11.

Kennedy, David. "Can We Still Afford to Be a Nation of Immigrants?" *The Atlantic Monthly* 278 (November 1996): 52–68.
   Argues in favor of immigration but sees the current situation as different from previous waves of immigration. Intelligent and well-reasoned but long.

Parrilo, Vincent. *Strangers to These Shores: Race and Ethnic Relations in the United States.* Boston–London: Allyn and Bacon, 1997.

Zwolinski, Matt. "Free Markets and Open Borders." *The Thinker* 4. April 30, 1997 <http://www.stanford.edu/group/Thinker/v4/n5/zwolinski.html>.
   An intelligent argument in favor of immigration written by a Stanford student.

Cluster 2: What Does It Mean to Be a Good American Citizen?

The problem of defining what it means to be a good citizen can emerge in such seemingly common activities as voting or expressing political opinions. It may be that these more mundane acts of citizenship give Americans cause to wonder about the relationship between their duties as citizens and their religious or ethnic loyalties.

Reading 1

Balzar, John. "Needed: Informed Voters." 2002. READING LEVEL 9.7.

Notes that political commentators routinely lament low voter turnouts, suggesting that low participation in American political campaigns ultimately weakens democracy. Balzar believes not only that voting is a right but that it also entails responsibility; in his view, it isn't enough simply to show up at the polling place to vote. Citizenship requires more.

Teacher to Teacher

This is a relatively simple and compelling read. The questions provided help both with careful reading and identifying Balzar's writing strategies.

ADDITIONAL DISCUSSION QUESTIONS

1. Paraphrase paragraph 11, which is central to understanding Balzar's argument. What do you learn about Balzar's position from this paragraph?

2. What do we learn from political advertisements?

3. Identify Balzar's tone by citing examples of charged language. Is his tone effective? What are some ways in which his tone might be considered offensive to some readers? Is his tone effective?

4. Have you ever voted? Is the activity of voting valued and promoted among your friends and family? How does your experience of voting (or not voting) affect your reading of this argument?

Reading 2

Baker, Russ. "Want to Be a Patriot? Do Your Job." 2002. READING LEVEL 12.0.

Baker believes that American journalists do have a responsibility as citizens. But he defines that responsibility in terms of the constitutional guarantee of a free press, which he views as fundamental to American democracy. In making his argument, Baker challenges not only journalists but all of us to define what we really mean by the term patriot.

Teacher to Teacher

This piece is directed toward journalists, so the slant provides an opportunity to focus on how one varies his writing for a specific, known audience. Some of the questions help students situate their own beliefs in response to those of Baker.

ADDITIONAL DISCUSSION QUESTIONS

1. Do you read or watch the news? Are you skeptical of journalists? What has helped inform your opinion of journalists? Did Baker's essay change your mind about journalism?

2. What does Baker think is the purpose of journalism? What do you think is the purpose of journalism?

3. Freedom of the press is a right guaranteed by our government. However, some limits are placed on what can be reported to protect national security. Should information be "managed" by the government? If so, what are the rules you would suggest for such management?

Reading 3

McClay, Wilfred M. "America: Idea or Nation?" 2001. READING LEVEL 12.0.

In this carefully reasoned essay, McClay makes it clear that because understanding America as an idea and as a nation can be challenging, patriotism is also a challenging concept. Explores what it means to be a patriot in a nation that is a powerful symbol of democracy both for its own citizens and for citizens of other nations. Also explores the symbolic importance of America refusing to simplify the issue of patriotism. The complexity of his argument may be appropriate, because McClay believes many Americans have not thought carefully about what it means to be a patriotic citizen.

Teacher to Teacher

This exceptionally long essay will likely interest students. Help students see how the marginalia provides support for and dimension to McClay's article. Use the questions, most of which students could answer on their own for homework, to analyze McClay's thinking. This would make a good piece on which to base a classroom debate.

1. What does the term *patriotic* mean to you? Is your definition of the term the same or different from McClay's? Do you consider yourself to be patriotic?

2. What are the assumptions that McClay seems to hold about America and about Americans?

3. This article was published in the Fall 2001 edition of *The Public Interest*, which likely means that it was written and sent off for publication prior to the September 11, 2001, attacks. Surely, the issues McClay raised here changed abruptly in the wake of those attacks. What parts of his argument are still valid today?

Reading 4

Kazin, Michael. "A Patriotic Left." 2002. READING LEVEL 12.0.

Kazin suggests that Americans with leftist political views not only seem to regularly endure the accusation of being unpatriotic, but also reject patriotism itself as a kind of blind loyalty to the U.S. Whether it is true or not that left-leaning Americans are more commonly charged with being unpatriotic than their fellow citizens with more moderate or conservative views, Kazin believes that patriotism is an important element in political debate. As an avowed leftist, he refuses to accept the criticism that leftists are unpatriotic because of their willingness to question their government. For Kazin, patriotism is something much more complicated than loyalty or love of country. It involves a deep sense of duty founded on the moral and ethical principles implicit in the U.S. Constitution.

Teacher to Teacher

This lengthy essay provides an interesting contrast to the McClay piece. The questions would make a good homework assignment to prepare students for a classroom discussion on this essay.

1. Who is Kazin's intended audience (see the sidebar on *Dissent* magazine)? How would this argument differ if it were directed to the readers of a conservative magazine?

2. Why does Kazin have to argue that people with "leftist" politics need to become patriotic?

3. Kazin takes issue with Martha Nussbaum's ideas about global citizenship. What is his concern about her argument?

4. At the end of his essay, Kazin invokes the words of Langston Hughes and identifies him as a "black, homosexual, and communist sympathizer." What is the effect of his using those words to describe Hughes?

5. How do you describe your own political stance? How do your politics affect the reading of this article?

Because we have The Bill of Rights, Americans typically know what their rights are. Write a letter to the editor of your college or local newspaper in which you put forth a proposal for the *responsibilities* of American citizens. Should responsibilities be stated concretely or abstractly? Should all Americans be required, for example, to vote and do community service? Should all Americans be allowed to choose not to do these things?

ADDITIONAL SUGGESTED READINGS

Allen, W. B. "The Good Citizen." The Philadelphia Society Fall Regional Meeting, Amway Grand Plaza Hotel, Grand Rapids, Michigan. 11 November 2000 <http://www.msu.edu/~allenwi/presentations/Good_Citizen.htm>.

Schudson, Michael. "Good Citizens and Bad History: Today's Political Ideals in Historical Perspective." "The Transformation of Civic Life" Conference. Middle Tennessee State University Murfreesboro and Nashville, Tennessee. 12–13 November 1999 <http://www.mtsu.edu/~seig/paper_m_schudson.html>.

Schudson, Michael. "What If Civic Life Didn't Die?" *The American Prospect* 25 (March–April 1996): 17–20 <http://epn.org/prospect/25/25-cnt1>.

Williams, Patricia J. "For Which We Stand." *The Nation* May 20, 2002.

Cluster 3: What Kind of Power Should We Give Our Government?

The essays in this section reveal some of the ways in which Americans have confronted the question of what "life, liberty, and the pursuit of happiness" means. As a group, these essays provide various perspectives on the relationship between a government and its citizens.

Reading 1

King, Martin Luther, Jr. "Letter from a Birmingham Jail" READING LEVEL 10.3.

"Letter from Birmingham a (the) Jail" was written in 1963, when King was jailed for eight days as the result of his campaign against segregation in Birmingham, Alabama. In the letter, King responds to white clergymen who had criticized his work and blamed him for breaking the law. A well-reasoned and carefully argued defense of civil disobedience as a means of securing civil liberties. In justifying his refusal to obey what he believed were unjust laws, King invokes a high moral standard by which to judge a government's actions.

Teacher to Teacher

This is a long but compelling essay with wide-ranging references to religion, politics, and ethics. The questions will help students comprehend the text and understand how King used these references to reach his audience.

1. King responds to the criticism that his campaign for civil rights was "untimely." What is his defense against this charge?

2. Why did King believe that a direct-action campaign was necessary in Birmingham? Why did the Black community in Birmingham turn to King? What problems were they facing, and what methods had they already tried before deciding on direct action?

3. What was the 1954 Supreme Court decision that King refers to in paragraph 16? Why was King able to charge that the "rabid segregationist" breaks the law?

4. King's critics charged that he obeyed the law selectively. He answers by arguing there is a difference between just and unjust laws. Do you, personally, agree with this distinction? How can you tell the difference between laws that you should honor and laws that you should break?

5. How does King characterize himself in this letter? What sort of a man does he seem to be, and what role does his presentation of himself play in this argument? How does he establish that he is someone worth listening to—and that it is important to listen to what he has to say?

Reading 2

Kelly, Michael. "Liberties Are a Real Casualty of War." 2002. READING LEVEL 12.0.

Some critics argue that in times of crisis Americans must guard their constitutional rights most jealously, for it is the guarantee of those rights that make America what it is. Kelly discusses such concerns as they emerged after 9-11. Referring to the case of Abdullah al Muhajir (formerly Jose Padilla), an American citizen who was held as a terrorist without formal charges, without a lawyer, and without a trial—a case that, according to critics, illustrated the dangers of too much government power over individual rights, Kelly staunchly believes that national security sometimes means sacrificing individual liberties. His argument raises the question as to whether such a sacrifice is warranted or whether it represents a government overstepping the constitutional limits of its power.

Teacher to Teacher

This is a short essay that will interest most students. Questions help students analyze the writer's strategies. This would make an interesting topic for class discussion on the power we grant to our government.

1. As more information about the detention of suspected terrorist operatives in the U.S. and abroad becomes available, does Kelly's argument become weaker or stronger?

2. Are you willing to forgo any of your personal liberties for the sake of national security? Which ones? If you aren't willing to forgo your personal liberties, explain why.

3. In Kelly's first paragraph, he interjects the highly informal, "oh, all right, spy upon." Read aloud, this makes his tone sound fairly humorous. What do you think about the effectiveness of this device?

4. Kelly is a conservative and is very much in favor of the policies of the Bush Administration. Show examples from the text of how a reader can infer this.

5. Explain why it is (or isn't) an effective parallel for Kelly to liken the loss of civil liberties to the draft.

Reading 3

Green, Heather. "Databases and Security vs. Privacy." 2002. READING LEVEL 12.0.

Green sees in national ID cards the potential for the abuse of the privacy of individual Americans. Points out that the debate over national ID cards is really a broader debate about the extent to which Americans are willing to sacrifice rights to privacy for greater security in a dangerous world, shows how the controversy over ID cards is also part of a debate about how much power the government should have over its citizens.

Teacher to Teacher

This is an essay that considers the issue of information gathering from a wider perspective than "should we or shouldn't we have ID cards." The careful reading questions will be important in helping students make the necessary connections to comprehend this piece.

ADDITIONAL DISCUSSION QUESTIONS

1. Does America need a clear definition of terrorism as Green says? Do we have such a definition already?

2. How would you characterize Green's attitude toward the U.S. government's methods of protecting national security? Do you share her views?

3. What do you think of the idea of creating national ID cards? What uses of surveillance, if any, would you personally support? Why?

Reading 4

Dershowitz, Alan M. "Why Fear National ID Cards?" 2001. READING LEVEL 11.5.

Dershowitz prefers "a system that takes a little bit of freedom from all to one that takes a great deal of freedom and dignity from the few" and believes that a national ID card is a worthwhile trade-off.

Teacher to Teacher

This essay provides an interesting contrast to the Heather Green piece. You might consider pairing the two for one class discussion. Use the questions to help students focus on how Dershowitz crafted his essay and made his point.

ADDITIONAL DISCUSSION QUESTIONS

1. Philosophers Jeremy Bentham and James Mill supported the idea of "utilitarianism," the idea that choices should always be made to effect the greatest happiness for the greatest number of people. Dershowitz plays on this idea in his article. Are libertarianism and utilitarianism ideas that co-exist well together? How?

2. For whom do you think Dershowitz was writing this piece? Who would most likely be convinced by the support he provides?

3. Dershowitz notes that legal immigrants would benefit from having the cards because it would help them "demonstrate their status to government official." Is this really a benefit? What are some opposing arguments to this one that you can think of?

4. With Dershowitz's point in mind that "American taxpayers, voters and driver long ago gave up any right of anonymity without loss of our right to engage in lawful conduct within zones of privacy," consider your experiences with anonymity, privacy and freedom in the U.S. How are anonymity, privacy, and freedom limited in the U.S.?

5. In paragraph 6, he calls this a "decentralized" country. What does this imply?

6. How plausible do you think the limits Dershowitz proposes for ID cards are? Can ID cards protect civil liberties, or are they are a risk to personal rights?

7. Is the fact that, as he notes in paragraph 7 there is already too much information "in the system" really an issue separate from this argument, as he says it is?

ALTERNATIVE WRITING ACTIVITY

Consider what national security requires of the average citizen. Should individual citizens give up rights, such as the right to privacy, in order to protect our country from terrorists? The Patriot Act is a recent bill that allows the government more powers than ever to protect its interests. Use the Internet to research this act—look for multiple viewpoints on this piece of legislation. Once you find out what powers The Patriot Act gives the government and how commentators have reacted to the act, write a response that states your position on the provisions of this act.

ADDITIONAL SUGGESTED READINGS

Brasch, Walt. "Ashcroft's Assault on Bookstores: The Fiction Behind National Security." *Counterpunch* July 25, 2002 <http://www.counterpunch.org/brasch0725.html>.
> *Earnest argument that the recent Patriot Act will result in implicit self-censorship on the part of publishers and booksellers who wish to avoid running afoul of government efforts to protect national security through the act.*

Kuttner, Robert. "Got Plastic? A Case for National ID Cards." *The American Prospect* May 6, 2002 <http://www.prospect.org/webfeatures/2002/05/kuttner-r-05-06.html>.
> *Well-written argument in favor of national ID cards as a way to guard against excessive government power over individuals.*

12 Free Enterprise

Cluster 1: What Is a Free Market?

As the essays in this chapter reveal, free markets do not exist apart from our social, cultural, and political lives, and these aspects of our lives complicate not only how markets work but also how we manage them. As a result, arguments about the moral and ethical aspects of free markets have become ever more complex, as economies grow and evolve and as new technologies create new possibilities and problems. In addition, many people continue to wonder whether free markets, no matter how efficiently they are run, really do make our lives better.

Reading 1

Wilder, Barbara. "Greed Despoils Capitalism." 2002. READING LEVEL 10.1.

Wilder responds to a columnist who believes that capitalism breeds successful businesspeople who have no conscience. Acknowledges that such businesspeople exist, but argues that capitalism requires not greed but ethical business practices. Otherwise, we all lose.

Teacher to Teacher

The basic comprehension questions provided with this reading are especially important for students who have not been introduced to economic principles. Using the excerpt from Adam Smith's *The Wealth of Nations* will help a bit with filling in this gap in student's knowledge.

ADDITIONAL DISCUSSION QUESTIONS

1. What do you think is the purpose of Wilder's opening statement: "I could never be accused of supporting President Bush"? What effect does it render?

2. In the second paragraph, Wilder refers to "the social contract." What does this mean?

3. What is the tone of this argument? Is it effective?

Reading 2

Mathews, Don. "The True Spirit of Enterprise." 2002. READING LEVEL 9.1.

Argues that people like Ford and Carnegie reflect the true spirit of free enterprise. Presents a view of the free market that emphasizes the entrepreneur and the idea of individual initiative.

ADDITIONAL DISCUSSION QUESTIONS

1. Mathews begins with the question *Does business run on greed?* How would you have answered that question prior to reading his argument? How would you answer it after reading it?

2. Do you agree with Mathews's statement at the end of the argument that "the drive to create and build that is the true spirit of enterprise"?

3. Using the complication "Robber Barons of the Gilded Age," discuss other ways of viewing the men whom Mathews cites as "giants."

Reading 3

Heath. Joseph, and Andrew Potter. "The Rebel Sell: If We All Hate Consumerism, How Come We Can't Stop Shopping?" 2002. READING LEVEL 9.5.

Article presents the idea that there's more to being a consumer than personal choice. Argues that the choices consumers make have far-reaching consequences that make our picks much more than personal preference. Argues that the backlash against consumerism in recent years, led by advocacy groups that emphasize the damage that a consumer culture can do to society, to the environment, and to our individual lives may miss the point. Views consumer culture as arising not just from the desire to acquire material goods, as many advocacy groups claim, but also from a deeply rooted desire among Americans to be different, to set themselves apart as individuals.

ADDITIONAL DISCUSSION QUESTIONS

1. How do you answer the questions with which Heath and Potter begin their essay?: Do you hate consumer culture? Angry about all that packaging? Irritated by all those commercials? Worried about the quality of the "mental environment"?

2. Examine the NoLogo and Adbusters Web sites and consider the ideas they present. Do you agree with their basic premises?

3. As a class, watch *Fight Club* or *American Beauty* and discuss the ways in which the films address consumer culture.

Reading 4

Korten, David. "Economies of Meaning." 1995. READING LEVEL 12.0.

Economist and activist David Korten is one influential voice in a growing chorus that questions the belief in the free market as a means to a better society for all. Looks carefully at the values that seem to drive the development of a global free market and argues that those values are not consistent with the good life so many people hope for. In particular, examines what he believes are myths about free markets—myths that lead to policies and business practices that undermine rather than foster justice and economic stability for the majority of people worldwide.

Teacher to Teacher

Because fewer students will be familiar with this subject matter, the higher reading level of this piece may prove more daunting than reading pieces of similar complexity on familiar topics. However, this is an interesting piece that is organized in such a way as to invite readers' comprehension. Have a discussion in which you help make connections between the items in the margins with the points Korten raises. Definitely assign all the questions, but you might want to have students answer them in small groups.

ADDITIONAL DISCUSSION QUESTIONS

1. Korten takes on a number of political stances. He takes issue with neoliberals, libertarians, and ideologues from both right and left. What do you think is Korten's political stance? What is the effect of his examination of these other ways of seeing?

2. Korten writes, "economic policies driven by these deeply flawed moral premises create a self-fulfilling prophecy by rewarding dysfunctional behaviors deeply detrimental to the healthy function of human societies, as we now see demonstrated all around us." Does he provide enough evidence to support this statement? What is your reaction to this statement?

ALTERNATIVE WRITING ASSIGNMENT

A free market economy is difficult to understand through simply reading four articles on the subject. Have students get into small groups and discuss the basics of what a free market economy is and what the alternatives to a free market would be. (You might want them to do some very simple and cursory research on the Internet.) Have the groups share their thoughts with the class so that all students have had a chance to think about this complicated topic. Once they are fairly comfortable speaking about general economic systems, assign the groups to create a proposal that outlines the basic way in which an "ideal" system of economics would be enacted in a country.

Ehrenreich, Barbara. "The Collapse of Credibility." *The Progressive* August 2002 <http://www.progressive. org/August%202002/ehr0802.html>.

Harsh, Lynn. "Capitalism—A Deal with the Devil?" *The Evergreen Freedom Foundation* November 2002 <http://www.effwa.org/newsletter/2002_11b.php>.

Hood, John. "Capitalism Saves: How Becoming an Investor Can Transform a Person—and a Nation." *The American Enterprise* July/August 2003 <http://www.theamericanenterprise.org/taeja02f.htm>.

Huffington, Arianna. "Capitalism without Conscience." *Common Dreams News Center* July 23, 2002 <http://www.commondreams.org/views02/0723-07.htm>.

Nader, Ralph. "Corporate Socialism." *Washington Post* July 18, 2002 <http://www.commondreams.org/ views02/0718-02.htm>

Tracinski, Robert W. "The Moral Basis of Capitalism." *The Center for the Advancement of Capitalism* <http://www.moraldefense.com/Philosophy/Essays/The_Moral_Basis_of_Capitalism.htm>.

Woiceshyn, Glenn. "Protection of Individual Rights Is Good Government." *Capitalism Magazine* April 5, 1998 <http://www.capmag.com/article.asp?ID=38>.

Cluster 2: What Does It Mean to Be a Consumer?

Conspicuous consumption raises questions about the decisions individuals make in spending their money. Do we really have the right to spend our money in any way we please, without regard to possible consequences? Is the kind of excessive consumption featured on television shows something that people should aspire to in a society that includes some people who are desperately poor? In other words, what responsibilities, if any, do consumers have?

The essays in this cluster reveal that there are many different answers to such questions. All these arguments suggest that buying things as consumers may not be as straightforward as we may think.

Reading 1

Frazier, Ian. "All-Consuming Patriotism: American Flag: $19.95. New Yacht: $75,000. True Patriotism? Priceless." 2002. READING LEVEL 9.0.

Frazier examines this connection between consumption and patriotism. Although poking fun at this connection, makes a serious point about what it means to be a consumer and a patriot.

Teacher to Teacher

This is an engaging, funny, and compelling piece of reading. It will likely lead to a lively discussion in the classroom.

ADDITIONAL DISCUSSION QUESTIONS

1. How do you, personally, relate to Frazier's experiences? Do your own experiences cause you to agree or disagree with his argument?

2. Compare the ideas in Frazier's argument with those of David Korten. How do these articles complement one another?

Reading 2

Deacon, James. "The Joys of Excess." 2002. READING LEVEL 10.8.

Describes some of the spending habits of wealthier citizens of Canada, a nation whose economy and culture are in many ways similar to those of the United States. Although critical of excessive spending on consumer goods by Canadians, avoids simply judging consumers. Interested in understanding why consumers engage in conspicuous consumption. Raises questions about the implications of such consumption—especially when it involves items that can obviously damage the environment, such as fuel-inefficient SUVs. In asking why such consumption occurs, explores the complicated issue of what it means to be a consumer.

Teacher to Teacher

This piece meshes well with the Frazier piece. It is another easy read. Because they are straightforward, you can assign the questions for homework. Be sure to refer students to the Adam Smith excerpt in the first cluster.

ADDITIONAL DISCUSSION QUESTIONS

1. Discuss how the words of Adam Smith (in the context for Cluster 1 of this chapter) can inform your reading of this argument.

2. Characterize Deacon's tone in this article. Given his tone, to whom do you think he is addressing this article?

3. Deacon notes the ways people are able to amass the wealth they display, such as having "both parents working." What effect does this detail have on you as a reader?

Reading 3

Solomon, Norman. "Mixed Messages Call for Healthy Skepticism." 2003. READING LEVEL 11.8.

Examines the contradictory messages conveyed by the news media, especially when it comes to issues such as health. For Solomon, these contradictory messages aren't just a reason for consumers to be skeptical of media reports; but also reflect a more fundamental problem in the media industry. As Solomon sees it, the media help create the very health problems they report on, in large part because they support products that are unhealthy and environmentally destructive.

Teacher to Teacher

This is an interesting and short read. It brings in the issue of the effects of advertising, which students are likely to have addressed in school before. The questions help analyze Solomon's argument.

1. What do you think is the role of advertising and media in the average person's life?

2. Does Solomon do enough to prove that "journalists routinely go easy on proven causes of cancer, such as cigarettes and an array of commercially promoted chemicals with carcinogenic effects"?

3. Solomon clearly thinks that the media that informs much of American life provides us with destructive messages. Does he offer any alternatives? If you believe, like Solomon, that our mass media needs to be changed, what alternatives would you suggest?

Reading 4

Singer, Peter. "The Singer Solution to World Poverty." 1999. READING LEVEL 10.5.

Well-known ethicist and philosopher Peter Singer believes that people who are economically comfortable have a responsibility for the economic plight of others who may be less fortunate; moreover, he has calculated exactly what that responsibility is in dollar figures. Examines how much money an average person in the United States must have to provide for basic needs. Any additional money, he asserts, is unnecessary and should be used to alleviate the pressing problem of world poverty.

Teacher to Teacher

This is a truly unusual piece of writing. Singer espouses a philosophy that will surely be engaging to most students. The questions will help students think carefully about Singer's proposal and see how he uses logic to get to his point. Answering the questions for homework should probably precede a class discussion on this essay.

ADDITIONAL DISCUSSION QUESTIONS

1. Do you believe in giving money to charitable organizations? Why? In your opinion, do people have a moral responsibility to help those in need?

2. What are the objections to Singer's argument that you could imagine people in the middle class making? What objections would wealthy individuals have to this argument?

ALTERNATIVE WRITING ASSIGNMENT

Consider the notion of consumerism. How do you feel about the ways in which citizens of our country are persuaded toward and engaged in purchasing material goods? Are there ethical standards to which consumers should adhere? Are there ethical standards to which advertisers should adhere? Write an essay directed toward other people your age in which you state your position and defend your reasoning.

Center for Consumer Freedom. 2003 <http://www.consumerfreedom.com/>.

Giroux, Henry A. "Animating Youth: The Disunification of Children's Culture." 1995 <http://www.gseis. ucla.edu/courses/ed253a/Giroux/Giroux2.html>.

Klein, Naomi. Transcript of Interview with Mick O'Regan *The Media Report* Thursday, January 17, 2002 <http://www.abc.net.au/rn/talks/8.30/mediarpt/stories/s445871.htm>.

Cluster 3: How Should Workers Be Treated?

The problems associated with labor conditions are not always straightforward. In some cases, the wages paid to factory workers in developing nations, which seem pitifully low by American standards, are actually lucrative compared to other workers in those nations. Moreover, in some regions, child labor is not looked upon as exploitation in the same way that it is in the United States. These issues highlight the complexities of questions about fair wages and ethical labor practices. What exactly is a "fair wage"? How do we decide? *Who* decides?

Reading 1

Kristof, Nicholas. "Let Them Sweat." 2002. READING LEVEL 12.0.

Argues that sweatshops, which have become a dirty word in many Western nations, can actually benefit the very same workers that advocacy groups describe as "exploited." Writing in the summer of 2002, when representatives of the world's leading economic powers—the "G-8"—were preparing to meet in Canada, Kristof cites examples of individual workers to illustrate the potential benefits of sweatshops. Urges the G-8 leaders to look carefully at such examples and accuses anti-sweatshop activists of ignoring the realities of the lives of the people they claim to be helping. In doing so, he reminds us that when it comes to working conditions and fair wages, what might be "exploitation" in one context may be something very different in another.

Teacher to Teacher

This short essay provides a different approach to the discussion about sweat-shops. It is an excellent contrast to anti-sweatshop essays in this cluster. The questions will help the students understand its implications. A good class discussion could result from using this piece paired with Hightower's.

ADDITIONAL DISCUSSION QUESTIONS

1. Are there alternatives to sweatshops that Kristof fails to consider? What are they?

2. Examine the Web sites of some anti-sweatshop groups to see how the information they provide meshes with or contradicts the details on which Kristof rests his argument.

Reading 2

Hales, Linda. "Rugmaking, Interwoven with Social Justice." 2002. READING LEVEL 10.4.

Points out that the vast majority of consumers admit that they wouldn't change their decisions about buying an item even if they knew the item was produced in a sweatshop or by child labor. Examines some efforts to encourage companies to buy products that are certified to have been made by workers who have not been exploited. Such efforts, especially by a non-profit organization called Rugmark, are an attempt to use the free market to foster social change. As Hales writes at the end of her essay, "In an imperfect world, there are no easy answers, only questions waiting be asked."

Teacher to Teacher

The questions for this easy-to-read essay help students see how Hales weaves an emotional appeal into her reasoning. This is a compelling essay that uses examples that will surely interest students.

ADDITIONAL DISCUSSION QUESTIONS

1. Compare Hales's premises with those of Kristof.

2. Thoughtful consumers who wish to buy responsibly—goods which Hales calls "politically correct," such as environmentally-friendly, organic, and sweatshop-free goods—are often made to feel guilty by such stories as those related by Hales in this article. What are some long- and short-term problems you can see with using this tactic of persuasion?

Reading 3

Hightower, Jim. "Going down the Road." 2002. READING LEVEL 12.0

Paying workers less money may be good for companies. That's one reason political observer Jim Hightower believes that the problem of sweatshops won't be addressed by government regulations intended to force businesses to treat workers better. Proposes an alternative approach: using the free market itself to create demand for goods that are produced in socially responsible ways. Using the example of a company called SweatX, Hightower argues that companies can compensate workers adequately and still realize profits. In effect, Hightower suggests that business success and social improvement can go hand-in-hand.

Teacher to Teacher

Hightower's essay employs sophisticated vocabulary and syntax, but it will be accessible to students because of the content. The questions are designed to link his ideas to the larger context.

1. Hightower invokes an occasionally humorous tone in this article, using such words as "globaloney" and calling President Bush "King George the W." What effect did this have on you? What effect might this have on someone who does not share your political viewpoint?

2. Compare the ideas behind Rugmark and SweatX. Are they similar? How do they differ?

Reading 4

Richards, Cindy. "Just Another Hollow Day." 2002. READING LEVEL 10.2.

> *Uses the occasion of the Labor Day holiday to examine the condition of working Americans in the first few years of the twenty-first century. She is concerned that as membership in labor unions has declined since the middle of the nineteenth century, so have the fortunes of the average worker. For Richards, Labor Day is a sad reminder of the influence that labor unions once had—but no longer do—to improve the working lives of Americans.*

Teacher to Teacher

Short, sweet essay that will be very readable for students. The questions will provide what they need to comprehend and analyze the piece.

ADDITIONAL DISCUSSION QUESTION

- What do you know about labor unions? What experiences with labor unions do you bring to the reading of this article that inform your understanding of it?

ALTERNATIVE WRITING ASSIGNMENT

You work in a factory situated in an urban area that employs approximately 250 workers. Recently, the corporate management has undergone a change, and workers have noticed major differences in their hours and working conditions. Some people have been regularly required to work double shifts, while other people, who once worked full time, are now working for hourly wages on a part-time basis. Health insurance has been completely revoked. Vacation time, sick leave, and personal days have been cut down. To cut costs, the security guards have been let go, allowing the parking lot and doors to go unmonitored despite the high crime rate in the neighborhood. These changes have affected all manner of workers from production to lower-management.

You and your co-workers are not in a union but have formed a committee to draft a letter to the management to express your concerns. Write a letter to the management of your company explaining what you consider to be fair working conditions.

Ehrenreich, Barbara, and Frances Fox Piven. "Who's Utopian Now?" *The Nation* 4 February 2002 <http://www.thenation.com/doc.mhtml?i=20020204&s=ehrenreich>.

Feldstein, Martin. "Reducing Poverty, Not Inequality." *The Public Interest* 137 (Fall 1999) <http://www.thepublicinterest.com/archives/1999fall/article2.html>.

13 Globalization

Cluster 1: Is Globalization Progress?

Globalization refers to a general trend toward more numerous and intimate connections between nations around the world. For many, globalization is primarily an economic phenomenon. Globalization also refers to the rapid increase of cross-cultural exchange, driven in part by powerful new communications technologies and media and by increased international travel. For many, globalization represents great opportunity and progress.

But globalization has a growing number of critics. For some critics, globalization represents not opportunity but the growing power of multinational corporations and the dominance of American consumer culture at the expense of local cultures. It means that people have less control as more and more aspects of their lives seem to be determined by distant economic and cultural forces. This cluster highlights these complexities. Each essay makes an argument about some aspect of globalization: economic, cultural, political, social.

Reading 1

Yergin, Daniel. "Giving Aid to World Trade." 2002. READING LEVEL 12.0.

One of the most persistent criticisms of economic globalization is that it contributes to poverty, particularly in developing nations whose populations are already poor. Some critics point out that as multinational corporations take advantage of relaxed international trade policies to increase their business in developing nations, they exploit resources at the expense of local populations. Yergin, a leading proponent of globalization, argues that such criticisms miss the point. Maintains that globalization offers opportunities for poorer nations to reap the same benefits that wealthier nations enjoy. The key, according to Yergin, is greater access to international trade, so that developing nations can become successful participants in the world marketplace. Their success, in turn, will lead to prosperity for their citizens.

Teacher to Teacher

The debates over globalization seem entirely too convoluted to many students, but it's important that they become informed about the issues. This essay is a good place to begin. Because of the complexity of the reading, the questions provided may work best if they are answered in small groups.

ADDITIONAL DISCUSSION QUESTIONS

1. Yergin's argument is founded on the idea that the economies of all countries are interconnected. The point he makes—by citing examples such as South Korea's and Singapore's successes—is that

globalization, handled well, could increase the health, education, and welfare of people in under-developed countries. Do these examples prove effective in helping him make his argument?

2. What counter-arguments does he refute in this article? What counter-arguments does he fail to acknowledge?

Reading 2

Norberg-Hodge, Helena. "The March of the Monoculture." 1999. READING LEVEL 12.0.

> *Points out that globalization not only results in economic change, but can also have a profound and dev-astating impact on local cultures. Where many advocates of globalization see great benefits in the increased availability of consumer goods in remote places, Norberg-Hodge sees the loss of distinctive and vibrant ways of life. In this sense, she suggests, the costs of globalization may far outweigh its benefits.*

Teacher to Teacher

This article extrapolates from the basic mechanisms of globalization and focuses on culture. Once students are grounded in the basic ideas of globalization, this will be an interesting piece to read with them. The examples she provides will be compelling for students. The questions are designed to help with careful reading. Some could be completed as homework assignments, others will need to be discussed in class.

ADDITIONAL DISCUSSION QUESTIONS

1. How does the use of historical exposition strengthen or weaken Norberg-Hodge's argument?

2. Norbert-Hodge writes, "Today, as wealth is transferred away from nation states into the rootless casino of the financial markets, the destruction of cultural integrity is far more subtle than before. Corporate and government executives no longer consciously plan the destruction they wreak—indeed they are often unaware of the consequences of their decisions on real people on the other side of the world. This lack of awareness is fostered by the cult of specialisation that pervades our society: the job of a public relations executive is confined to producing business-friendly sound bites, while time pressures and a narrow focus prevent a questioning of their overall impact. The tendency to undermine cultural diversity proceeds, as it were, on 'automatic pilot' as an inevitable consequence of the spreading global economy." This paragraph appears to make more than one point. Paraphrase this paragraph and then outline the points she makes. Examine the point she makes regarding specialization. How does her example of the public relations executive function to make this point?

3. By using phrases such as "in diverse 'developing' nations around the world," Norbert-Hodge reveals her assumptions. What assumptions appear to underlie her argument?

4. What parts of this argument might be considered contradictory? How could these contradictions be resolved?

Reading 3

Shiva, Vandana. "The Living Democracy Movement: Alternatives to the Bankruptcy of Globalisation." 2002. READING LEVEL 12.0.

In this challenging essay, human rights and environmental activist Shiva, a physicist critic of globalization, argues that the policies of international organizations like the WTO are not only economic measures, but they also reflect philosophical, political, and ecological beliefs that are not shared by the world population. For Shiva, the process of globalization that is fueled by such policies is bankrupt because it reduces the complex needs of human beings to commodities. In rejecting globalization, Shiva transforms the issue from an economic one to a human one. Her argument reminds us that the growing debates about globalization are intense precisely because the stakes are so high.

Teacher to Teacher

Shiva's piece provides a contrast the Yergin piece. You might consider assigning this one before the Norberg-Hodge one. The questions are comprehensive.

ADDITIONAL DISCUSSION QUESTION

- Compare Shiva's premises to those of Yergin.

Reading 4

Claeson, Bjorn Skorpen. "Singing for the Global Community." 2002. READING LEVEL 11.6.

Bjorn Skorpen Claeson puts a human face on the concerns so often heard in protests against globalization. Describes a different kind of event that occurred in Bangor, Maine, in the summer of 2002: a concert and fair intended not only to publicize the plight of the workers whose lives have been harmed by globalization, but also to celebrate these same workers and the global community we are all part of. Essay may seem idealistic and perhaps even romantic, but his argument about what it means to be part of a world that is increasingly interdependent is not so easy to dismiss.

Teacher to Teacher

This is a short and easy-to-read essay that makes a very emotional appeal. The questions are activity-oriented and might make good group projects.

ADDITIONAL DISCUSSION QUESTION

- Compare the argumentation tactics of Claeson with those of Yergin.

Write a letter to the editor in which you state your position on the sale and purchase of goods made in sweatshops.

ADDITIONAL SUGGESTED READINGS

Diamond, Jared. "Why We Must Feed the Hands That Could Bite Us." *The Washington Post* 13 January 2002: B01 <http://www.washingtonpost.com/ac2/wp-dyn?pagename=article&node=&contentId=A34805-2002Jan12&notFound=true>.

Galbraith, James K. "The Crisis of Globalization." *Dissent* 46, 3, Summer 1999.

Graham, Carol. "Can Foreign Aid Help Stop Terrorism? Not With Magic Bullets." *The Brookings Review*, 20, 3. Summer 2002.

O'Neill, Brendan. "When Nation-Building Destroys." *Spiked-online* 4 April 2002 <http://www.spiked-online.com/Articles/00000006D87C.htm>.

Cluster 2: What Is Fair Trade?

When trade involves goods that cross international borders, many different laws and policies can come into play. Solutions are never easy to find. But solutions will need to be found, because the question of what constitutes fair trade is a vitally important one. It relates not only to the prices we pay for goods but also to the responsibilities we all have as consumers. In that respect, fair trade is of concern to all of us.

Reading 1

Hewitt, Patricia. "Free Trade for a Fair, Prosperous World." READING LEVEL 9.9.

Free trade and fair trade are not the same thing. In fact, many critics of globalization and of the economic policies of large capitalist nations like the United States argue that truly free trade can never be fair because free trade ultimately means that some people will suffer. Hewitt, a proponent of free trade believing that it will lead to fair and prosperous conditions for workers, provided that it is conducted ethically, lays out her vision for ethical free trade. In the process, she offers a vision of fairness in trade as well, and she challenges businesspeople—and especially those who support globalization—to accept their responsibilities for fostering fairness in the marketplace.

Teacher to Teacher

This is an interesting piece to teach because it was prepared as a speech. Note that the reading level is low, which is a obviously a result of its original purpose. That leads to a good opportunity to discuss with students the constraints of having to deliver an argument orally.

- What assumptions regarding the lives of those in other countries appear to underlie Hewitt's argument? Compare Hewitt's assumptions with those of Norberg-Hodge's in cluster one of this chapter. How do these two writers disagree?

Reading 2

Ransom, David. "Fair Trade: Small Change, Big Difference." 2000. READING LEVEL 10.5.

Ransom, a vigorous opponent of globalization and an advocate of fair trade, argues that fair trade can be an important element in the growing effort to counteract globalization, and he describes many of the benefits of fair trade. But he acknowledges the drawbacks of fair trade as well, not the least of which is the small impact it has made so far in the global marketplace.

Teacher to Teacher

This is a slightly longer piece, but the reading level makes it accessible. The questions are intended to help with careful reading and evaluation of how the argument fits in the larger dialogue.

ADDITIONAL DISCUSSION QUESTIONS

1. Ransom makes claims in his argument that are not supported by evidence. Identify the claims he makes that are effective and the ones that are ineffective. What kinds of information would need to be presented for you to consider the claims effective?

2. Ransom's conclusion is less formal than other portions of the article. What are the effects of ending the article this way?

Reading 3

Jagger, Bianca. "Squeezed to the Last Drop." 2002. READING LEVEL 12.0

As globalization reshaped international markets, the coffee industry began to experience changes that led to labor conflicts as well as to environmental controversies. Coffee suppliers began to buy large quantities of coffee from growers in Central and South America, which led to changes in growing and labor practices—changes that many critics claimed were unfair to workers and damaging to the environment. But despite its popularity, coffee decreased in price, and the industry as a whole suffered. Bianca Jagger reports that no one has suffered more than the small coffee growers themselves. She traces the problem to the practices of large corporations involved in the coffee trade, and she calls for support of fair trade coffee as a solution.

Teacher to Teacher

This is a fairly short essay that provides a concrete example that is likely to help students see the issue of globalization more clearly. Questions will help students make personal connections to the reading as well as analyze Jagger's rhetoric

- Compare and contrast the argumentation strategies Jagger uses to those of Ransom in the previous essay.

Reading 4

North, Rodney. "Finding Meaning in a Cup of Coffee." 2001. READING LEVEL 8.3.

Advocates fair trade as a way to address the serious economic and environmental problems in the coffee industry from the perspective of a businessperson. Working for Equal Exchange, a business organization that promotes fair trade in coffee, North argues that business success and the principles of fair trade can be achieved at the same time.

Teacher to Teacher

This easy-to-read article is an excellent companion to both the Ransom and Jagger pieces. Questions are straightforward and would work as a homework assignment prior to class discussion.

ADDITIONAL DISCUSSION QUESTIONS

1. Bianca Jagger and Rodney North have the same agenda, but they are approaching different audiences with their arguments. Compare and contrast the ways in which the two writers address their audiences.

2. In his article in this cluster, David Ransom notes that a problem with fair trade stores that nags him is that "fair-trade products still cost more to buy and so are apparently aimed at people like me who can just about afford them." North's proposal offers a different way of approaching fair trade. How would this approach alleviate the problem that nags Ransom?

ALTERNATIVE WRITING ASSIGNMENT

Are there any fair-trade stores where you live? As Ransom points out, these stores typically sell traditional crafts and coffee. If you have ever visited a fair-trade store, do you remember what the store sold? If you haven't visited such a store, you might consider going to take a look around and get some literature on the store's guiding philosophy. Is the selection wide enough to cause you to return to this store? What are the positive aspects of having a store like this in your community? What are the drawbacks?

Write an argument to inquire in which you consider the reasons for supporting such a store in your community. If your community does not house such a business, you might consider making your argument a proposal for or against inviting one to open in your town.

Castro, Max. "US Policy Toward Latin America Ignores Poverty, Disparity." *Miami Herald* July 16, 2002 <http://www.commondreams.org/views02/0716-08.htm>.

Saunders, Paul J. "Why 'Globalization' Didn't Rescue Russia." *Policy Review Online* 105 (February/March 2001) <http://www.policyreview.org/feb01/saunders.html>.

William, Easterly. "The Cartel of Good Intentions." *Foreign Policy* <http://www.foreignpolicy.com/issue_julyaug_2002/Easterly.html>.

Cluster 3: How Should We Share the Earth?

Global warming, the depletion of fish populations in the world's oceans, and the environmental destruction caused by energy use, especially fossil fuels, are global problems that affect all the earth's residents. They are also social, cultural, and ethical challenges. It also makes them extremely difficult to solve. And to address these challenges requires us to confront the question, *How should we share our earth?*

Reading 1

Herbert, Bob. "No Margin for Error." 2002. READING LEVEL 11.6.

Columnist Bob Herbert is chiefly concerned with what the consequences of rising global temperatures will be. He describes the apparent effects of global warming on one crucial ecosystem: the earth's oceans. Herbert knows that scientists and policy-makers disagree about the extent of global warming and its impact. But he argues that the potential for catastrophic environmental damage is so great that we cannot waste time debating any longer.

Teacher to Teacher

Most students will be familiar with this type of argument, and its topic is sure to elicit strong responses from students. The questions help them analyze his rhetoric.

ADDITIONAL DISCUSSION QUESTION

- In newspapers, editors often comment on information that is created by others. In this article, Herbert relies heavily on findings of a study done by Oppenheimer and O'Neill. Realizing that Herbert is relying on the information reported by others, how would you approach the reading of this piece?

Reading 2

Balling, Robert C., Jr. "The Global Warming Scapegoat." 2002. READING LEVEL 12.0.

Balling, an expert on climate and geology, believes that the debates about climate change themselves are part of the problem. Examines how misconceptions about the relationship between climate change and recent weather events, such as hurricanes and tornadoes, lead to misleading press reports about global warming. Argues that the scientific evidence does not support what is often reported in the press. Although he does not dismiss the possibility that the earth's atmosphere is indeed warming, he urges caution in how we make sense of the available scientific data.

Teacher to Teacher

This is an excellent contrast to the piece by Herbert. The argument is offered with a political agenda likely to be unfamiliar to students, who are more likely to be familiar with the global warming hypothesis. The questions will help students examine Balling's rhetorical strategy.

ADDITIONAL DISCUSSION QUESTION

- Read the mission statement of International Policy Network. What can be inferred about the biases of this group and how they are implicit in Balling's argument?

Reading 3

Kwegsi. "Injustice? Duress and the Burnt Church First Nation Fisheries Agreement with Canada." 2002. READING LEVEL 10.8.

In the 1990s, the Esgenoôpetitj, or Burnt Church, First Nation of Nova Scotia found themselves fighting to retain their traditional fishing and lobstering rights in the face of confusing legal decisions and violent attacks by non-native residents. Kwegsi, a leader of the Burnt Church First Nation, discusses this conflict, arguing that it is another instance of a longstanding effort by the Canadian government to deny First Nation peoples their rights.

Teacher to Teacher

This is a straightforward, easy read and provides another concrete example of how environmental concerns of some come into direct conflict with the political and cultural concerns of others. Definitely assign this one in concert with the ones by Herbert and Balling.

ADDITIONAL DISCUSSION QUESTIONS

1. Kwegsi directly blames the Canadian government for the violence against the native fishermen. Is this emotional appeal effective? Does he offer sufficient proof for this assertion?

2. Are rights such as fishing native waters inherent? Should natives of a country be automatically afforded rights that "settlers" have to attain through government permission?

Reading 4

Mitra, Barun. "Stop Energy EcoImperialism." 2002. READING LEVEL 12.0.

Mitra is concerned about the effects of globalization on the health of the environment, especially in his native India. But he is convinced that what is good for the economy is also good for the environment, and he argues vigorously in favor of free market policies that, he believes, will lead to economic growth in developing nations like India. Rejects the efforts of western activists who claim to support environmental protection in developing nations, calling such activism "eco-imperialism." In his view, people in developing nations like India should have access to the same economic benefits that are available to industrialized nations like the U.S.

Teacher to Teacher

This piece is more complex than the other ones in this cluster, and it provides a more philosophical response to what Mitra perceives as an encroachment *of* Indians' rights by environmental activists. The questions help situate the piece in the larger dialogue and may be well suited for small group work.

ADDITIONAL DISCUSSION QUESTIONS

1. What is the reason Mitra is opposed to renewable energy? Is his reason clearly stated in his article?

2. Are Greenpeace and the Body Shop's efforts to influence the ways in which energy is generated appropriate? What are Mitra's objections to this campaign? Do organizations such as Greenpeace have a right to interfere with the decisions of countries on how to generate energy for their people?

ALTERNATIVE WRITING ASSIGNMENT

Imagine you live in a community that has recently learned that its groundwater and soil have been contaminated by runoff from a factory that was owned seventy years ago by a family business that has long since closed and the building torn down. No one can legally be held responsible for the pollution. Selling your house is not an option, as the contamination has driven away all potential buyers. Neither you nor anyone else in the neighborhood is able or willing to simply abandon your houses. You need help from your local government to work out this problem in a fair and equitable way. Write a letter addressed to your representative in state or local government that explores the situation in which you find yourselves.

Bray, Thomas J. "Scorched Earth Policy: Environmentalists Would Still Rather See Forests Burn for the Trees." *Wall Street Journal Opinion Journal* August 27, 2002 <http://opinionjournal.com/columnists/tbray/>.

Hunter, Natasha. "Too Predictable: The New Republic Swats at Environmentalists, but Misses a Few Facts." *The American Prospect* May 2, 2002 <http://www.prospect.org/webfeatures/2002/05/hunter-na-05-02.html>.